A Book of Anagrams – An Ancient Word Game: Volume 2

Daniel H. Wieczorek

A Book of Anagrams – An Ancient Word Game: Volume 2

ISBN-10: 1470015528
ISBN-13: 978-1470015527

DEDICATION

Dedicated to my Mother – who always encouraged me to have an interest in words, vocabulary, dictionaries and reading and always made sure that, of the limited budget available, some part of it was to be used for books. Thanks Mom.

Also dedicated to the Sisters, Servants of the Immaculate Heart of Mary, who taught me at Saints Peter and Paul School when I was a youngster – their dedication to teaching to the highest standards also encouraged me to take a very deep interest in reading, vocabulary and words. Their continual insistence of, "go to the dictionary", when we did not know the meaning of a new word surely gave me a deep respect for vocabulary and dictionaries.

Other books by Daniel H. Wieczorek include:

A Book of Anagrams – An Ancient Word Game
(Print and E-book Editions)

Outdoor Photography of Japan: Through the Seasons
(co-authored with Kazuya Numazawa)
(Print and E-book Editions)

Some Violets of Eastern Japan
(co-authored with Kazuya Numazawa)
(Print and E-book Editions)

English – Ilokano And Ilokano – English Dictionary
(Print and E-book Editions)

These titles are all available through your local bookseller (search the internet for the appropriate ISBN's) or through Amazon.

FOREWORD

What is an anagram? An anagram is a rearrangement of the letters of one word or phrase to form another word or phrase. In this work you will find sixty-one 9-letter words which have been disassembled and the letters placed in a grid. It's your job to find as many words as you can in the scrambled 9 letters and in so doing, also find the original 9-letter word. In addition, in this 2nd volume you will find four 12-letter words which have been disassembled and the letters placed in a grid. It's your job to find as many words as you can in the scrambled 12 letters and in so doing, also find the original 12-letter word.

A web search for the history of anagrams will give you many more results than you want to read. Let it suffice to say that they have been around for a LONG TIME! It seems that they've been around since at least the 3rd century BC and the Greek poet Lycophron. It also seems that anagrams were believed to have mystical or prophetic meaning in some eras of history. In the Middle Ages, anagrammatists often entertained, by creating witty anagrams of people's names.

For the anagrams which are listed in this work, the Anagrams tool of the CD-ROM version of the 3rd Edition of the American Heritage Dictionary was used. Several results for each word were then deleted – for example abbreviations such as ROM, RAM, UNESCO, DOS, CPU, ECT, EEG and so on. Capitalized words which were repeats of lowercase words were usually deleted – for example Red, Trine, Host, Sir and so on. It was felt that a single entry (lowercase) was enough. Please forgive me if you find more words – the edition of the American Heritage Dictionary which was used was created in 1993, it is an older version and may not have the newest words. You may occasionally find an abbreviation which I failed to delete, they were not intentionally left here, but were discovered by reviewers.

Also, please forgive the use of different size fonts on the various results pages. It was desired to fit the results for each word on a single page and therefore a font size was used which permitted this.

The base word (the real word) from which each anagram was created is underlined on each results page. In some cases, when it is felt the reader may not know the word, the definition of the base word has been included on the results page.

By the way, while you work, for example, on Anagram #2 you will be able to see the results list from Anagram #1, so it is suggested that you use your hand or a piece of paper to cover that result list while you work on the following anagram so as to not give yourself hints and clues. There were two alternatives available for showing the results pages – either immediately after each anagram, or all of the results pages at the end of the book. It seemed that the alternative selected was the best way to go.

When you see a grid similar to the one below – the shaded "A", and the fact that it is in a heavily outlined box – this indicates that the letter "A" must be used in every word you make.

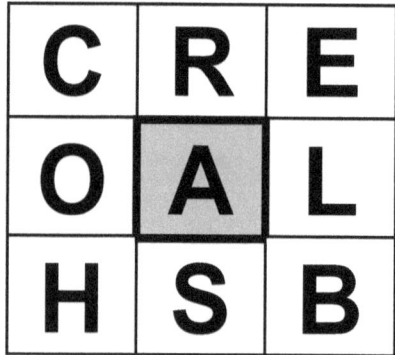

If there is no shaded nor heavily outlined letter in a grid then it indicates that there is no letter which must be used in every word.

TABLE OF CONTENTS

#1

How many words can you make from these 9 letters?
There is no letter which must be used in every word.
You can use only these 9 letters and a letter cannot be
used more than once in any word (you may use 2 A's
and 2 E's). It's possible to make one 9-letter word.
Score: 20 words or more – EXCELLENT
    15 words or more – VERY GOOD
    10 words or more – GOOD
Hint: don't forget the plural forms of words, for example
ant is 1 word and ants is a 2nd word. It's possible to
make 148 words of 3 or more letters. (See following
page for answers).

A	E	M
S	E	T
A	B	N

Your Answers: _____ _____ _____

_____ _____ _____ _____

_____ _____ _____ _____

_____ _____ _____ _____

_____ _____ _____ _____

_____ _____ _____ _____

_____ _____ _____ _____

_____ _____ _____ _____

This page _____ _____ _____
Photocopiable _____ _____ _____

1. abase	39. bean	77. mat	115. seamen
2. abasement	40. beans	78. mate	116. seat
3. abate	41. beast	79. mates	117. see
4. abates	42. beat	80. mats	118. seem
5. abeam	43. beaten	81. mean	119. seen
6. abet	44. beats	82. meanest	120. semen
7. abets	45. bee	83. means	121. sen
8. absent	46. been	84. meant	122. senate
9. ameba	47. bees	85. meat	123. sent
10. amebas	48. beet	86. meet	124. set
11. amen	49. beets	87. meets	125. stab
12. ant	50. bent	88. men	126. stamen
13. ante	51. bents	89. mesa	127. steam
14. antes	52. beset	90. met	128. stem
15. ants	53. best	91. mete	129. tab
16. Asante	54. bet	92. metes	130. tabs
17. ate	55. beta	93. nab	131. tame
18. baa	56. bets	94. nabs	132. tames
19. baas	57. ease	95. nae	133. tan
20. ban	58. east	96. name	134. tans
21. bane	59. eat	97. names	135. tea
22. bans	60. eaten	98. neat	136. team
23. bantam	61. eats	99. neb	137. teams
24. bantams	62. emanate	100. nebs	138. teas
25. base	63. emanates	101. nee	139. tease
26. baseman	64. enema	102. nest	140. tee
27. basemen	65. enemas	103. net	141. teem
28. basement	66. man	104. nets	142. teems
29. bast	67. manatee	105. samba	143. teen
30. baste	68. manatees	106. same	144. teens
31. bat	69. mane	107. sane	145. tees
32. bate	70. manes	108. sat	146. ten
33. bates	71. mans	109. Satan	147. tens
34. bats	72. manse	110. sate	148. tense
35. batsman	73. manta	111. sateen	This page
36. batsmen	74. mantas	112. sea	Photocopiable
37. beam	75. mantes	113. seam	
38. beams	76. mast	114. seaman	

a·base (ə-bās′) *tr.v.* **a·based**, **a·bas·ing**, **a·bas·es**. To lower in rank, prestige, or esteem. -- **a·base′ment** *n.*

2

#2

How many words can you make from these 9 letters? There is no letter which must be used in every word. You can use only these 9 letters and a letter cannot be used more than once in any word (you may use 2 A's and 2 T's). It's possible to make one 9-letter word.

Score: 20 words or more – EXCELLENT

15 words or more – VERY GOOD

10 words or more – GOOD

Hint: don't forget the plural forms of words, for example oar is 1 word and oars is a 2nd word. It's possible to make 142 words of 3 or more letters. (See following page for answers).

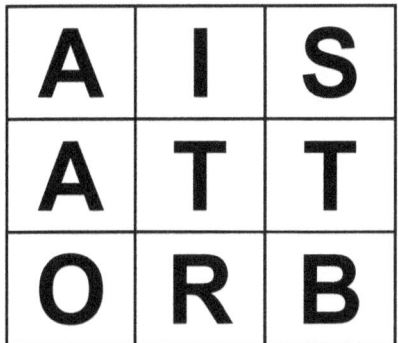

Your Answers:

1. abattoir	37. boar	73. rats	109. Tai
2. abattoirs	38. boas	74. rib	110. Tais
3. abort	39. boast	75. ribs	111. Taoist
4. aborts	40. boat	76. riot	112. tar
5. air	41. boats	77. riots	113. taro
6. airs	42. bra	78. roast	114. taros
7. aorta	43. bras	79. rob	115. tarot
8. aortas	44. brat	80. robs	116. tarots
9. Arab	45. brats	81. rot	117. tars
10. Arabs	46. brio	82. rots	118. tarsi
11. aria	47. Brit	83. sabra	119. tart
12. arias	48. Brits	84. sari	120. tarts
13. art	49. Ibo	85. sat	121. tat
14. artist	50. iota	86. sir	122. tats
15. arts	51. isobar	87. sit	123. tiara
16. astir	52. its	88. sitar	124. tis
17. atria	53. oar	89. soar	125. tit
18. attar	54. oars	90. sob	126. tits
19. attars	55. oat	91. sort	127. toast
20. baa	56. oats	92. sot	128. tor
21. baas	57. obi	93. stab	129. tori
22. bait	58. obis	94. stair	130. tors
23. baits	59. obit	95. star	131. torsi
24. bar	60. orb	96. start	132. tort
25. bars	61. orbit	97. stat	133. torts
26. bast	62. orbits	98. stir	134. tot
27. bat	63. orbs	99. stoa	135. tots
28. bats	64. ottar	100. stoat	136. trait
29. bias	65. ottars	101. strait	137. traits
30. bio	66. Rabi	102. strata	138. trio
31. bios	67. Rabia	103. strati	139. trios
32. biota	68. Rabias	104. stria	140. trot
33. bistro	69. Rabis	105. tab	141. trots
34. bit	70. rat	106. tabor	142. tsar
35. bits	71. ratio	107. tabors	
36. boa	72. ratios	108. tabs	

ab·at·toir (ăb′ə-twär′) *n.* **1.** A slaughterhouse. **2.** Something likened to a slaughterhouse.

4

#3

How many words can you make from these 9 letters? There is no letter which must be used in every word. You can use only these 9 letters and a letter cannot be used more than once in any word (you may use 2 A's and 2 C's). It's possible to make one 9-letter word.

Score: 20 words or more – EXCELLENT

     15 words or more – VERY GOOD

     10 words or more – GOOD

Hint: don't forget the plural forms of words, for example ace is 1 word and aces is a 2nd word. It's possible to make 108 words of 3 or more letters. (See following page for answers).

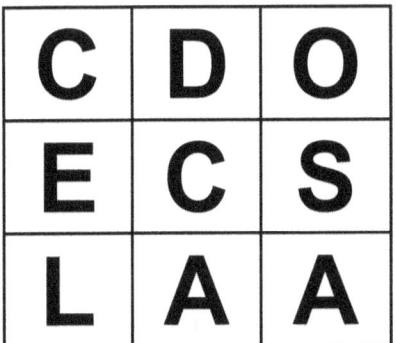

Your Answers:

1.	accolade	28.	clad	55.	dale	82.	lodes
2.	accolades	29.	clads	56.	dales	83.	lose
3.	ace	30.	cloaca	57.	deal	84.	ode
4.	aced	31.	cloacae	58.	deals	85.	odes
5.	aces	32.	clod	59.	decal	86.	old
6.	ado	33.	clods	60.	doe	87.	sac
7.	ads	34.	close	61.	does	88.	sad
8.	ala	35.	closed	62.	dole	89.	sal
9.	alae	36.	coal	63.	doles	90.	salad
10.	alas	37.	coaled	64.	dose	91.	sale
11.	ale	38.	coals	65.	lace	92.	scald
12.	ales	39.	coca	66.	laced	93.	scale
13.	aloe	40.	cocas	67.	laces	94.	scaled
14.	aloes	41.	cod	68.	lad	95.	scold
15.	also	42.	coda	69.	lade	96.	sea
16.	cacao	43.	codas	70.	lades	97.	seal
17.	cacaos	44.	code	71.	lads	98.	sec
18.	cad	45.	codes	72.	Lao	99.	sled
19.	cads	46.	cods	73.	Laos	100.	sloe
20.	caeca	47.	coed	74.	lea	101.	sod
21.	calces	48.	coeds	75.	lead	102.	soda
22.	cascade	49.	cola	76.	leads	103.	sol
23.	case	50.	colas	77.	led	104.	solace
24.	cased	51.	cold	78.	Leo	105.	solaced
25.	caseload	52.	colds	79.	load	106.	sold
26.	ceca	53.	dace	80.	loads	107.	sole
27.	cecal	54.	daces	81.	lode	108.	soled

ac·co·lade (ăk′ə-lād′, -läd′) *n.* **1.a.** An expression of approval; praise. **b.** A special acknowledgment; an award. **2.** A ceremonial embrace, as of greeting or salutation. **3.** Ceremonial bestowal of knighthood. -- **ac·co·lade** *tr.v.* **ac·co·lad·ed**, **ac·co·lad·ing**, **ac·co·lades**. To praise or honor.

6

#4

How many words can you make from these 9 letters? Every word must contain the letter "A". You can use only these 9 letters and a letter cannot be used more than once in any word (you may use 2 E's). It's possible to make one 9-letter word.

Score: 20 words or more – EXCELLENT

    15 words or more – VERY GOOD

    10 words or more – GOOD

Hint: don't forget the plural forms of words, for example raid is 1 word and raids is a 2nd word. It's possible to make 150 words of 4 or more letters. (See following page for answers).

Your Answers:

1. adverse	39. datives	77. rates	115. Tais
2. advert	40. davit	78. rats	116. tare
3. advertise	41. dear	79. rave	117. tared
4. adverts	42. dearest	80. raved	118. tares
5. advise	43. dears	81. raves	119. tars
6. aerie	44. deviate	82. read	120. tarsi
7. aeries	45. deviates	83. readies	121. tear
8. aide	46. diva	84. readiest	122. teared
9. aider	47. divas	85. reads	123. tears
10. aides	48. eared	86. said	124. teas
11. aids	49. ears	87. sari	125. tease
12. aired	50. ease	88. sate	126. teased
13. airs	51. eased	89. sated	127. teaser
14. Ares	52. easier	90. satire	128. tirade
15. arid	53. east	91. save	129. trade
16. Aries	54. Easter	92. saved	130. trades
17. arise	55. eater	93. saver	131. tread
18. arts	56. eats	94. sear	132. treads
19. aside	57. eaves	95. seared	133. triad
20. aster	58. erase	96. seat	134. tsade
21. astir	59. erased	97. seated	135. tsar
22. astride	60. evade	98. sedate	136. varied
23. aver	61. evader	99. sedative	137. varies
24. avers	62. evades	100. sitar	138. vase
25. averse	63. idea	101. staid	139. vast
26. avert	64. ideas	102. stair	140. vaster
27. averted	65. ideate	103. star	141. vats
28. averts	66. ideates	104. stare	142. Veda
29. avid	67. irate	105. stared	143. Vedas
30. dais	68. rads	106. starve	144. Vesta
31. dare	69. raid	107. starved	145. visa
32. dares	70. raids	108. stave	146. visaed
33. dart	71. raise	109. staved	147. visard
34. darts	72. raised	110. stead	148. vista
35. date	73. rase	111. steadier	149. vita
36. dater	74. rased	112. stria	150. vitae
37. dates	75. rate	113. striae	
38. dative	76. rated	114. tads	

#5

How many words can you make from these 9 letters? There is no letter which must be used in every word. You can use only these 9 letters and a letter cannot be used more than once in any word. It's possible to make one 9-letter word.

Score: 20 words or more – EXCELLENT

     15 words or more – VERY GOOD

     10 words or more – GOOD

Hint: don't forget the plural forms of words, for example flea is 1 word and fleas is a 2nd word. It's possible to make 166 words of 4 or more letters. (See following page for answers).

Your Answers:

1. aegis	43. fine	85. haling	127. naifs
2. ages	44. fines	86. hang	128. nail
3. agile	45. fins	87. hangs	129. nails
4. ails	46. fish	88. Hans	130. neigh
5. aisle	47. flag	89. heal	131. neighs
6. ales	48. flags	90. healing	132. nigh
7. alien	49. flan	91. heals	133. nighs
8. aliens	50. flange	92. hens	134. safe
9. align	51. flanges	93. hinge	135. sage
10. aligns	52. flash	94. hinges	136. sail
11. aline	53. flashing	95. ilea	137. sale
12. alines	54. flea	96. inhale	138. saline
13. angel	55. fleas	97. inhales	139. sane
14. angelfish	56. flesh	98. isle	140. sang
15. angels	57. fleshing	99. lags	141. seal
16. angle	58. flies	100. lain	142. sealing
17. angles	59. fling	101. lane	143. self
18. anise	60. flings	102. lanes	144. shag
19. ashen	61. Gael	103. lash	145. shale
20. easing	62. Gaels	104. lashing	146. sheaf
21. egis	63. gain	105. leaf	147. sheafing
22. English	64. gains	106. leafing	148. shelf
23. fags	65. gale	107. leafs	149. shin
24. fail	66. gales	108. lean	150. shine
25. fails	67. gals	109. leans	151. shingle
26. fain	68. gash	110. leash	152. sigh
27. false	69. geisha	111. leashing	153. sign
28. fang	70. gels	112. leasing	154. signal
29. fangs	71. genial	113. legs	155. silage
30. fans	72. gins	114. leis	156. sine
31. feign	73. glans	115. lens	157. sing
32. feigns	74. glean	116. liane	158. singe
33. fens	75. gleans	117. lianes	159. single
34. figs	76. glen	118. lief	160. slag
35. file	77. glens	119. lien	161. slain
36. files	78. gnash	120. lies	162. slang
37. fils	79. hags	121. life	163. sleigh
38. finagle	80. hail	122. linage	164. sling
39. finagles	81. hails	123. line	165. snag
40. final	82. hale	124. lines	166. snail
41. finale	83. hales	125. nags	
42. finals	84. half	126. naif	

#6

How many words can you make from these 9 letters? There is no letter which must be used in every word. You can use only these 9 letters and a letter cannot be used more than once in any word (you may use 2 R's). It's possible to make one 9-letter word.

Score: 20 words or more – EXCELLENT

     15 words or more – VERY GOOD

     10 words or more – GOOD

It's possible to make 148 words of 3 or more letters. (See following page for answers).

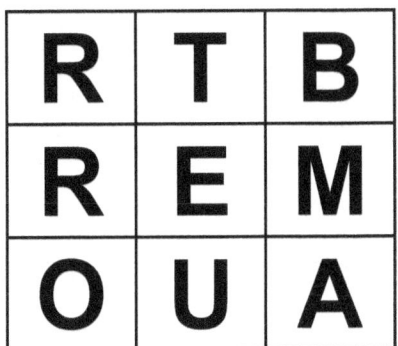

Your Answers:

1. abet	38. borate	75. oar	112. tabor
2. abort	39. bore	76. oat	113. tabour
3. about	40. bout	77. orate	114. tabu
4. abut	41. bra	78. orb	115. tame
5. amber	42. brat	79. ore	116. tamer
6. amour	43. bream	80. our	117. tar
7. arbor	44. brute	81. out	118. tare
8. arboretum	45. bum	82. outer	119. taro
9. are	46. bur	83. ram	120. tau
10. arm	47. buret	84. rare	121. tea
11. armer	48. burr	85. rat	122. team
12. armor	49. burro	86. rate	123. tear
13. armour	50. but	87. ream	124. term
14. art	51. buteo	88. rear	125. toe
15. arum	52. ear	89. reb	126. toea
16. ate	53. eat	90. rebut	127. tom
17. atom	54. emu	91. remora	128. tomb
18. auto	55. era	92. roam	129. tome
19. bar	56. err	93. roamer	130. tor
20. bare	57. erratum	94. roar	131. tore
21. barer	58. mar	95. rob	132. torr
22. barter	59. mare	96. robe	133. tour
23. bat	60. mart	97. roe	134. tourer
24. bate	61. mat	98. rot	135. tram
25. beam	62. mate	99. rote	136. tremor
26. bear	63. mature	100. rout	137. true
27. beat	64. meat	101. route	138. truer
28. beau	65. met	102. router	139. tub
29. beaut	66. moat	103. rub	140. tuba
30. berm	67. mob	104. rube	141. tube
31. bet	68. more	105. rue	142. tuber
32. beta	69. mortar	106. ruer	143. tumor
33. boa	70. mot	107. rum	144. umber
34. boar	71. mote	108. rumba	145. umbra
35. boat	72. moue	109. rumor	146. umbrae
36. boater	73. mute	110. rut	147. urea
37. Boer	74. muter	111. tab	148. Ute

ar·bo·re·tum (är′bə-rē′təm) *n.*, *pl.* **ar·bo·re·tums**
or **ar·bo·re·ta** (-tə). A place where an extensive variety
of woody plants are cultivated for scientific,
educational, and ornamental purposes.

12

#7

How many words can you make from these 9 letters? There is no letter which must be used in every word. You can use only these 9 letters and a letter cannot be used more than once in any word (you may use 2 A's and 2 R's). It's possible to make one 9-letter word.

Score: 20 words or more – EXCELLENT

15 words or more – VERY GOOD

10 words or more – GOOD

It's possible to make 101 words of 3 or more letters. (See following page for answers).

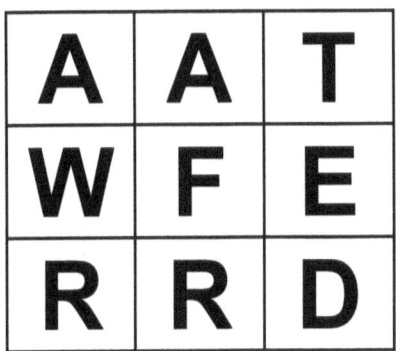

Your Answers:

1. afar	35. era	69. reward
2. aft	36. err	70. tad
3. after	37. errata	71. tar
4. <u>afterward</u>	38. fad	72. tare
5. are	39. fade	73. tarred
6. area	40. far	74. taw
7. art	41. farad	75. tea
8. ate	42. fare	76. tear
9. award	43. fared	77. trade
10. awarder	44. farer	78. trader
11. aware	45. fat	79. tread
12. awe	46. fate	80. wad
13. awed	47. fated	81. wade
14. daft	48. fear	82. wader
15. dafter	49. feat	83. wafer
16. dare	50. fed	84. waft
17. darer	51. feta	85. wafted
18. dart	52. few	86. wafter
19. darter	53. fret	87. war
20. data	54. rad	88. ward
21. date	55. radar	89. warder
22. dater	56. raft	90. ware
23. deaf	57. rafted	91. wared
24. dear	58. rafter	92. warfare
25. deft	59. rare	93. warred
26. dew	60. rat	94. wart
27. draft	61. rate	95. warted
28. draw	62. rated	96. water
29. drawer	63. raw	97. wear
30. drear	64. rawer	98. wed
31. drew	65. read	99. weft
32. dwarf	66. rear	100. wert
33. ear	67. red	101. wet
34. eat	68. retard	

#8

How many words can you make from these 9 letters? There is no letter which must be used in every word. You can use only these 9 letters and a letter cannot be used more than once in any word (you may use 2 A's and 2 R's). It's possible to make one 9-letter word.

Score: 20 words or more – EXCELLENT

    15 words or more – VERY GOOD

    10 words or more – GOOD

Hint: don't forget the plural forms of words, for example air is 1 word and airs is a 2nd word. It's possible to make 121 words of 3 or more letters. (See following page for answers).

Your Answers:

1. afar	42. farm	83. Rama
2. afire	43. farms	84. ramie
3. aim	44. fear	85. rams
4. aims	45. fears	86. rare
5. air	46. fie	87. rase
6. airfare	47. fir	88. ream
7. airfares	48. fire	89. reams
8. airframe	49. firearm	90. rear
9. airframes	50. firearms	91. rears
10. airs	51. firer	92. reis
11. amir	52. fires	93. rem
12. amirs	53. firm	94. rems
13. are	54. firmer	95. rife
14. area	55. firms	96. rifer
15. areas	56. firs	97. rim
16. Ares	57. frame	98. rime
17. aria	58. frames	99. rimer
18. arias	59. friar	100. rimers
19. Aries	60. friars	101. rimes
20. arise	61. frier	102. rims
21. arm	62. friers	103. rise
22. armer	63. fries	104. riser
23. armies	64. ifs	105. Safar
24. arms	65. ire	106. safari
25. arras	66. ism	107. safe
26. ars	67. mafia	108. safer
27. ear	68. mar	109. same
28. ears	69. mare	110. sari
29. emir	70. mares	111. sea
30. era	71. maria	112. seam
31. err	72. marries	113. sear
32. errs	73. mars	114. semi
33. fair	74. Masai	115. sera
34. fairer	75. maser	116. serf
35. fairs	76. mesa	117. serif
36. fame	77. mire	118. sierra
37. fames	78. mires	119. sir
38. far	79. miser	120. sire
39. fare	80. raise	121. smear
40. farer	81. raiser	
41. fares	82. ram	

#9

How many words can you make from these 9 letters? There is no letter which must be used in every word. You can use only these 9 letters and a letter cannot be used more than once in any word (you may use 2 A's). It's possible to make one 9-letter word.

Score: 20 words or more – EXCELLENT

     15 words or more – VERY GOOD

     10 words or more – GOOD

It's possible to make 188 words of 3 or more letters. (See following page for answers).

A	G	E
A	O	T
I	N	R

Your Answers:

1. aeon	48. gainer	95. Negro	142. rot
2. aerating	49. gait	96. net	143. rote
3. again	50. gaiter	97. nit	144. tag
4. agar	51. gar	98. niter	145. Tai
5. agate	52. garnet	99. nitre	146. taiga
6. age	53. gate	100. nor	147. Taino
7. agent	54. gater	101. not	148. tan
8. ager	55. gator	102. note	149. tanager
9. ago	56. gear	103. noter	150. tang
10. agora	57. gent	104. oar	151. tango
11. agorae	58. get	105. oaring	152. tar
12. aigret	59. giant	106. oat	153. tare
13. air	60. gin	107. ogre	154. taring
14. anger	61. girt	108. one	155. tarn
15. angora	62. gnat	109. orange	156. taro
16. ant	63. goat	110. orate	157. tea
17. ante	64. goiter	111. orating	158. tear
18. aorta	65. gone	112. ore	159. tearing
19. aortae	66. goner	113. organ	160. ten
20. <u>aragonite</u>	67. gore	114. orient	161. tenor
21. are	68. got	115. ornate	162. tern
22. area	69. grain	116. rag	163. tiara
23. arena	70. granite	117. rage	164. tie
24. argent	71. grant	118. rain	165. tier
25. argon	72. grate	119. ran	166. tiger
26. argot	73. great	120. rang	167. tin
27. aria	74. grin	121. range	168. tine
28. art	75. grit	122. rani	169. tinge
29. ate	76. groan	123. rant	170. tire
30. atone	77. groin	124. rat	171. toe
31. atoner	78. ignore	125. rate	172. toea
32. atria	79. inert	126. rating	173. toeing
33. ear	80. ingot	127. ratio	174. tog
34. earing	81. ingrate	128. ration	175. toga
35. earn	82. inter	129. regain	176. ton
36. eat	83. into	130. region	177. tone
37. eating	84. ion	131. reign	178. toner
38. ego	85. iota	132. rein	179. tonier
39. eon	86. irate	133. rent	180. tor
40. era	87. ire	134. retain	181. tore
41. erg	88. iron	135. retina	182. tori
42. ergo	89. nae	136. rig	183. torn
43. ergot	90. nag	137. ring	184. train
44. eta	91. naira	138. riot	185. triage
45. Gaea	92. near	139. rite	186. trig
46. Gaia	93. neat	140. roan	187. trine
47. gain	94. negator	141. roe	188. trio

a·rag·o·nite *n.*, (ə-răg′ə-nīt′, ăr′ə-gə-) A usually white, yellowish, or pink orthorhombic mineral that can occur in many different colors.

#10

How many words can you make from these 9 letters? There is no letter which must be used in every word. You can use only these 9 letters and a letter cannot be used more than once in any word (you may use 2 S's). It's possible to make one 9-letter word.

Score: 20 words or more – EXCELLENT

 15 words or more – VERY GOOD

 10 words or more – GOOD

Hint: don't forget the plural forms of words, for example seat is 1 word and seats is a 2nd word. It's possible to make 159 words of 4 or more letters. (See following page for answers).

T	S	U
S	E	I
O	P	A

Your Answers:

1. apes	41. pats	81. seas	121. step
2. apse	42. patsies	82. seat	122. steps
3. apses	43. pause	83. seats	123. sties
4. asps	44. pauses	84. sepia	124. stoa
5. asset	45. peas	85. sepias	125. stoae
6. atop	46. peat	86. septa	126. stoas
7. auto	47. peso	87. sets	127. stop
8. autopsies	48. pesos	88. setup	128. stops
9. autos	49. pest	89. setups	129. stoup
10. east	50. pesto	90. siesta	130. stoups
11. eats	51. pestos	91. sips	131. sues
12. iota	52. pests	92. site	132. suet
13. issue	53. pets	93. sites	133. suit
14. oases	54. pies	94. sits	134. suite
15. oasis	55. pious	95. soap	135. suites
16. oats	56. pita	96. soapiest	136. suits
17. opiate	57. piteous	97. soaps	137. sups
18. opiates	58. pits	98. sops	138. Tais
19. opts	59. Piute	99. sots	139. tape
20. opus	60. Piutes	100. soup	140. tapes
21. opuses	61. poet	101. soupiest	141. taps
22. oust	62. poets	102. soups	142. taupe
23. ousts	63. poise	103. souse	143. teas
24. outs	64. poises	104. spas	144. ties
25. paise	65. pose	105. spat	145. tips
26. Paiute	66. poses	106. spate	146. tissue
27. Paiutes	67. posies	107. spates	147. toea
28. paseo	68. posit	108. spats	148. toes
29. paseos	69. posits	109. spies	149. tops
30. pass	70. posse	110. spit	150. toss
31. past	71. post	111. spite	151. tossup
32. paste	72. posts	112. spites	152. Tupi
33. pastes	73. pots	113. spits	153. Tupis
34. pasties	74. pout	114. spot	154. upset
35. pasts	75. pouts	115. spots	155. upsets
36. pate	76. puss	116. spouse	156. uses
37. pates	77. puts	117. spout	157. Utes
38. patio	78. saps	118. spouts	158. utopia
39. patios	79. sate	119. sputa	159. utopias
40. patois	80. sates	120. stapes	

#11

How many words can you make from these 9 letters? Every word must contain the letter "A". You can use only these 9 letters and a letter cannot be used more than once in any word. It's possible to make one 9-letter word.

Score: 20 words or more – EXCELLENT

    15 words or more – VERY GOOD

    10 words or more – GOOD

Hint: don't forget the plural forms of words, for example crab is 1 word and crabs is a 2ⁿᵈ word. It's possible to make 165 words of 4 or more letters. (See following page for answers).

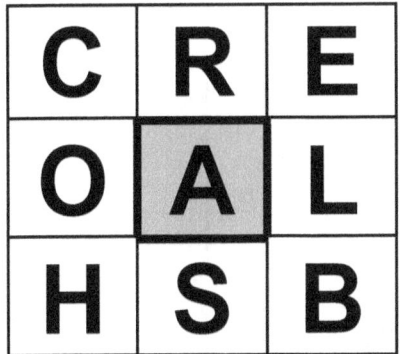

Your Answers:

1. abhor	43. boas	85. cola	127. oars
2. abhors	44. bola	86. colas	128. oracle
3. able	45. bolas	87. coral	129. oral
4. abler	46. boreal	88. crab	130. orca
5. acerb	47. brace	89. crabs	131. orcas
6. aces	48. braces	90. crash	132. race
7. ache	49. bras	91. each	133. races
8. aches	50. brash	92. earl	134. rase
9. acre	51. breach	93. earls	135. rash
10. acres	52. broach	94. ears	136. reach
11. albs	53. broaches	95. hale	137. real
12. ales	54. cable	96. haler	138. reals
13. aloe	55. cabler	97. halers	139. rhea
14. aloes	56. cables	98. hales	140. rheas
15. also	57. cabs	99. halo	141. roach
16. arch	58. care	100. haloes	142. roaches
17. arches	59. cares	101. halos	143. saber
18. arcs	60. carob	102. haole	144. sable
19. Ares	61. carobs	103. haos	145. sabre
20. arose	62. carol	104. hare	146. sale
21. ashore	63. carols	105. hares	147. scab
22. bachelor	64. cars	106. heal	148. scale
23. bachelors	65. case	107. heals	149. scar
24. bale	66. cash	108. hear	150. scare
25. baler	67. chaos	109. hears	151. scholar
26. bales	68. char	110. herbal	152. sclera
27. bare	69. chars	111. hoarse	153. seal
28. bares	70. chase	112. labor	154. sear
29. bars	71. chaser	113. labors	155. search
30. base	72. cholera	114. labs	156. sera
31. baser	73. choral	115. lace	157. shale
32. bash	74. chorale	116. lacer	158. share
33. basher	75. chorals	117. laces	159. shear
34. beach	76. chorea	118. Laos	160. shoal
35. bear	77. clash	119. larch	161. slab
36. bears	78. clear	120. larches	162. soar
37. blare	79. clears	121. laser	163. solace
38. blares	80. coal	122. lash	164. solacer
39. bleach	81. coals	123. leach	165. solar
40. blear	82. coarse	124. leash	
41. blears	83. cobra	125. loach	
42. boar	84. cobras	126. loaches	

#12

How many words can you make from these 9 letters? There is no letter which must be used in every word. You can use only these 9 letters and a letter cannot be used more than once in any word. It's possible to make one 9-letter word.

Score: 20 words or more – EXCELLENT

    15 words or more – VERY GOOD

    10 words or more – GOOD

Hint: don't forget the plural forms of words, for example face is 1 word and faces is a 2nd word. It's possible to make 186 words of 3 or more letters. (See following page for answers).

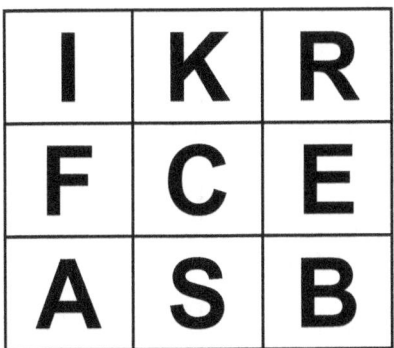

Your Answers:

1. ace	48. bier	95. fabric	142. rack
2. acerb	49. biers	96. fabrics	143. racks
3. aces	50. bike	97. face	144. raise
4. acre	51. biker	98. faces	145. rake
5. acres	52. bikers	99. fair	146. rakes
6. afire	53. bikes	100. fairs	147. rase
7. air	54. bra	101. fake	148. reb
8. airs	55. brace	102. fakes	149. rebs
9. arc	56. braces	103. fakir	150. rib
10. arcs	57. braise	104. far	151. ribs
11. are	58. brake	105. farce	152. rice
12. Ares	59. brakes	106. farces	153. rices
13. Aries	60. bras	107. fare	154. rick
14. arise	61. break	108. fares	155. ricks
15. ark	62. breaks	109. fear	156. rife
16. arks	63. brick	110. fears	157. rise
17. ascribe	64. bricks	111. fib	158. risk
18. ask	65. brief	112. fiber	159. saber
19. back	66. briefs	113. fibers	160. sabre
20. backer	67. brisk	114. fibre	161. sac
21. backers	68. cab	115. fibres	162. sack
22. backfire	69. cabs	116. fibs	163. safe
23. backfires	70. cafe	117. fie	164. safer
24. backs	71. cafes	118. fir	165. sake
25. bake	72. cake	119. fire	166. saki
26. bakes	73. cakes	120. fires	167. sari
27. bar	74. car	121. firs	168. scab
28. bare	75. care	122. freak	169. scar
29. bares	76. cares	123. freaks	170. scare
30. barf	77. Carib	124. fries	171. scarf
31. barfs	78. Caribs	125. frisk	172. scribe
32. baric	79. caries	126. ice	173. sea
33. bark	80. cars	127. ices	174. sear
34. barks	81. case	128. ifs	175. sec
35. bars	82. cask	129. ire	176. sera
36. base	83. ceiba	130. irk	177. Serb
37. baser	84. ceibas	131. irks	178. serf
38. basic	85. crab	132. Kaiser	179. serif
39. bask	86. crabs	133. kerb	180. sic
40. beak	87. creak	134. kerbs	181. sick
41. beaks	88. creaks	135. kerf	182. sicker
42. bear	89. crib	136. kerfs	183. sir
43. bears	90. cribs	137. Rabi	184. sire
44. beck	91. cries	138. rabies	185. ski
45. bias	92. ear	139. Rabis	186. skier
46. bicker	93. ears	140. race	
47. bickers	94. era	141. races	

#13

How many words can you make from these 9 letters? There is no letter which must be used in every word. You can use only these 9 letters and a letter cannot be used more than once in any word (you may use 2 E's and 2 T's). It's possible to make one 9-letter word.

Score: 20 words or more – EXCELLENT

    15 words or more – VERY GOOD

    10 words or more – GOOD

Hint: don't forget the plural forms of words, for example beet is 1 word and beets is a 2nd word. It's possible to make 194 words of 4 or more letters. (See following page for answers).

E	E	T
S	A	T
B	I	R

Your Answers:

1. abet	40. bears	79. ears	118. seat	157. teariest
2. abets	41. beast	80. ease	119. seer	158. tears
3. abetter	42. beat	81. easier	120. sera	159. teas
4. aerie	43. beats	82. east	121. Serb	160. tease
5. aeries	44. beer	83. Easter	122. sere	161. teaser
6. airs	45. beers	84. eater	123. setter	162. teat
7. Ares	46. bees	85. eats	124. sire	163. Tebet
8. Aries	47. beet	86. erase	125. sitar	164. Tebets
9. arise	48. beets	87. Erie	126. site	165. tees
10. artiest	49. berate	88. Eries	127. sitter	166. terse
11. artist	50. berates	89. Erse	128. stab	167. test
12. artiste	51. beret	90. estate	129. stair	168. tester
13. arts	52. beretta	91. ester	130. star	169. testier
14. aster	53. berettas	92. irate	131. stare	170. tetra
15. astir	54. beset	93. iterate	132. start	171. tetras
16. attire	55. best	94. iterates	133. stat	172. tier
17. attires	56. bestir	95. Rabi	134. state	173. tiers
18. bait	57. beta	96. rabies	135. steer	174. ties
19. baiter	58. bets	97. Rabis	136. stere	175. tire
20. baits	59. better	98. raise	137. stet	176. tires
21. bare	60. betters	99. rase	138. stir	177. titer
22. bares	61. bias	100. rate	139. strait	178. titers
23. barest	62. bier	101. rates	140. strati	179. titre
24. barite	63. biers	102. ratite	141. street	180. titres
25. bars	64. biretta	103. ratites	142. stria	181. tits
26. base	65. birettas	104. rats	143. striae	182. trait
27. baser	66. bite	105. rebate	144. tabs	183. traits
28. bast	67. biter	106. rebates	145. Tais	184. treat
29. baste	68. bites	107. rest	146. tare	185. treaties
30. baster	69. bits	108. ribs	147. tares	186. treatise
31. bate	70. bitter	109. rise	148. tars	187. treats
32. bates	71. bitters	110. rite	149. tarsi	188. tree
33. batiste	72. braise	111. rites	150. tart	189. trees
34. bats	73. bras	112. saber	151. tarts	190. tribe
35. batter	74. brat	113. sabre	152. taste	191. tribes
36. batteries	75. brats	114. sari	153. taster	192. tries
37. batters	76. breast	115. sate	154. tastier	193. trite
38. battier	77. Brit	116. satire	155. tats	194. tsar
39. bear	78. Brits	117. sear	156. tear	

#14

How many words can you make from these 9 letters? There is no letter which must be used in every word. You can use only these 9 letters and a letter cannot be used more than once in any word (you may use 2 A's and 2 L's). It's possible to make one 9-letter word.

Score: 20 words or more – EXCELLENT

    15 words or more – VERY GOOD

    10 words or more – GOOD

It's possible to make 143 words of 3 or more letters. (See following page for answers).

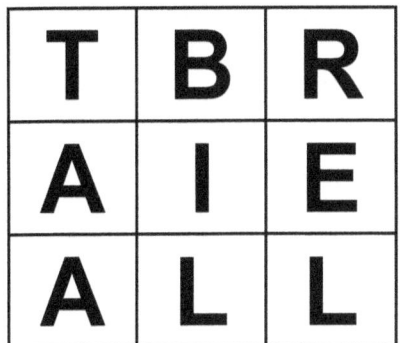

Your Answers:

1. abate	37. ball	73. ill	109. rial
2. abet	38. ballet	74. irate	110. rib
3. able	39. bar	75. ire	111. riel
4. abler	40. bare	76. lab	112. rile
5. aerial	41. barite	77. label	113. rill
6. ail	42. bat	78. labia	114. rille
7. air	43. bate	79. labial	115. rite
8. ala	44. bear	80. lair	116. tab
9. alae	45. beat	81. lariat	117. table
10. alb	46. bell	82. late	118. Tai
11. albeit	47. belt	83. later	119. tail
12. ale	48. bet	84. lateral	120. tala
13. alert	49. beta	85. lea	121. tale
14. alit	50. bier	86. lei	122. tali
15. all	51. bilateral	87. let	123. tall
16. altar	52. bile	88. liable	124. taller
17. alter	53. bill	89. liar	125. tar
18. Arab	54. billet	90. libel	126. tare
19. arable	55. bit	91. liberal	127. tea
20. are	56. bite	92. Libra	128. teal
21. area	57. biter	93. lie	129. tear
22. aria	58. blare	94. lilt	130. tell
23. aril	59. blear	95. lira	131. tiara
24. arillate	60. bleat	96. lire	132. tie
25. art	61. bra	97. lit	133. tier
26. ate	62. braille	98. liter	134. tile
27. atria	63. brat	99. literal	135. tiler
28. atrial	64. Brit	100. litre	136. till
29. baa	65. ear	101. Rabi	137. tiller
30. Baal	66. earl	102. Rabia	138. tire
31. bail	67. eat	103. rail	139. trail
32. bailer	68. ell	104. rat	140. trial
33. bait	69. era	105. rate	141. tribal
34. baiter	70. eta	106. real	142. tribe
35. bale	71. ilea	107. reb	143. trill
36. baler	72. ileal	108. retail	

bi·lat·er·al (bī-lăt′ər-əl) *adj.* **1.** Having or formed of two sides; two-sided. **2.** Affecting or undertaken by two sides equally; binding on both parties. **3.** Having or marked by bilateral symmetry. -- **bi·lat′er·al·ism** *n.* --**bi·lat′er·al·ly** *adv.* --**bi·lat′er·al·ness** *n.*

#15

How many words can you make from these 9 letters? There is no letter which must be used in every word. You can use only these 9 letters and a letter cannot be used more than once in any word (you may use 2 E's). It's possible to make one 9-letter word.

Score: 20 words or more – EXCELLENT

  15 words or more – VERY GOOD

  10 words or more – GOOD

Hint: don't forget the plural forms of words, for example ape is 1 word and apes is a 2nd word. It's possible to make 152 words of 3 or more letters. (See following page for answers).

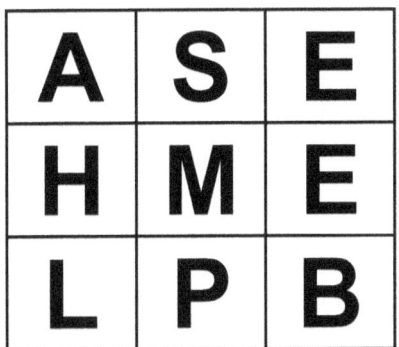

Your Answers:

1. able	39. bleeps	77. lames	115. peels
2. ahem	40. ease	78. lamp	116. pes
3. alb	41. easel	79. lamps	117. phase
4. albs	42. eel	80. lams	118. plash
5. ale	43. eels	81. lap	119. plasm
6. alee	44. elapse	82. laps	120. plea
7. aleph	45. elm	83. lapse	121. pleas
8. ales	46. elms	84. lash	122. please
9. alms	47. else	85. lea	123. pleb
10. alp	48. empale	86. leap	124. plebe
11. alps	49. hale	87. leaps	125. plebes
12. amble	50. hales	88. lease	126. plebs
13. ambles	51. ham	89. leash	127. psalm
14. amp	52. hams	90. lee	128. sable
15. ample	53. hap	91. lees	129. sale
16. amps	54. haps	92. male	130. same
17. ape	55. has	93. males	131. sample
18. apes	56. hasp	94. map	132. sap
19. apse	57. heal	95. maple	133. sea
20. ash	58. heals	96. maples	134. seal
21. asleep	59. heap	97. maps	135. seam
22. asp	60. heaps	98. mash	136. see
23. bale	61. heel	99. meal	137. seem
24. bales	62. heels	100. meals	138. seep
25. balm	63. helm	101. mesa	139. sepal
26. balms	64. helms	102. mesh	140. shale
27. base	65. help	103. pal	141. sham
28. bash	66. helps	104. pale	142. shamble
29. beam	67. hem	105. pales	143. shame
30. beams	68. heme	106. palm	144. shape
31. bee	69. hemp	107. palms	145. she
32. beep	70. hems	108. pals	146. sheep
33. beeps	71. lab	109. pas	147. shlep
34. bees	72. labs	110. pea	148. slab
35. blame	73. lam	111. peal	149. slam
36. blames	74. lamb	112. peals	150. slap
37. <u>blaspheme</u>	75. lambs	113. peas	151. sleep
38. bleep	76. lame	114. peel	152. spa

blas·pheme (blăs-fēm′, blăs′fēm′) *v.* **blas·phemed,
blas·phem·ing, blas·phemes.** --*tr.* **1.** To speak of (God or a
sacred entity) in an irreverent, impious manner. **2.** To revile;
execrate. --*intr.* To speak blasphemy. **--blas·phem′er** (blăs-
fē′mər, blăs′fə-) *n.*

#16

How many words can you make from these 9 letters? There is no letter which must be used in every word. You can use only these 9 letters and a letter cannot be used more than once in any word (you may use 2 I's). It's possible to make one 9-letter word.

Score: 20 words or more – EXCELLENT

    15 words or more – VERY GOOD

    10 words or more – GOOD

It's possible to make 94 words of 3 or more letters. (See following page for answers).

B	T	M
I	E	R
I	C	O

Your Answers:

1. berm	33. erotic	65. rice
2. bet	34. Ibo	66. rim
3. bier	35. ice	67. rime
4. bio	36. icier	68. riot
5. biome	37. ire	69. rite
6. biometric	38. item	70. rob
7. biotic	39. meiotic	71. robe
8. bit	40. merit	72. roe
9. bite	41. met	73. rot
10. biter	42. metric	74. rote
11. Boer	43. mice	75. term
12. bore	44. micro	76. tic
13. brim	45. microbe	77. tie
14. brio	46. mire	78. tier
15. Brit	47. mite	79. timber
16. cero	48. miter	80. timbre
17. cir	49. mitre	81. time
18. cite	50. mob	82. timer
19. cob	51. more	83. tire
20. comb	52. mortice	84. toe
21. comber	53. mot	85. tom
22. come	54. mote	86. tomb
23. comer	55. obi	87. tome
24. comet	56. obit	88. tor
25. core	57. omit	89. tore
26. corm	58. orb	90. tori
27. cot	59. orbit	91. tribe
28. cote	60. ore	92. trice
29. crib	61. reb	93. trim
30. crime	62. recto	94. trio
31. emir	63. remit	
32. emit	64. rib	

bi·o·met·rics (bī′ō-mĕt′rĭks) *n. (used with a sing. verb)*
1. The statistical study of biological phenomena. **2.** The measurement of physical characteristics, such as fingerprints, DNA, or retinal patterns, for use in verifying the identity of individuals. -- **bi′o·met′ric** , **bi′o·met′ri·cal** *adj.* **bi′o·met′ri·cal·ly** *adv.*

#17

How many words can you make from these 9 letters? There is no letter which must be used in every word. You can use only these 9 letters and a letter cannot be used more than once in any word. It's possible to make one 9-letter word.

Score: 20 words or more – EXCELLENT

     15 words or more – VERY GOOD

     10 words or more – GOOD

It's possible to make 171 words of 3 or more letters. (See following page for answers).

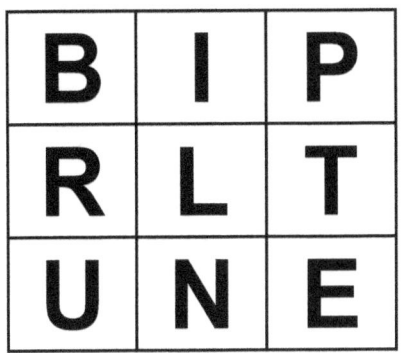

Your Answers:

1. belt	44. inure	87. pier	130. rune
2. bent	45. ire	88. pile	131. runlet
3. bet	46. lei	89. pin	132. runt
4. bier	47. lent	90. pine	133. rut
5. bile	48. let	91. pint	134. ten
6. bin	49. letup	92. pit	135. tern
7. bit	50. leu	93. Piute	136. tie
8. bite	51. lie	94. pleb	137. tier
9. biter	52. lien	95. plier	138. tile
10. blent	53. lieu	96. print	139. tiler
11. blip	54. line	97. prune	140. tin
12. blue	55. liner	98. pub	141. tine
13. blueprint	56. lineup	99. pul	142. tip
14. bluer	57. lint	100. pule	143. tire
15. blunt	58. lip	101. puler	144. tribe
16. blunter	59. lire	102. puli	145. tribune
17. blur	60. lit	103. pun	146. trine
18. blurt	61. liter	104. punier	147. trip
19. brine	62. litre	105. punt	148. tripe
20. Brit	63. lube	106. punter	149. triple
21. bruin	64. lupin	107. pure	150. true
22. bruit	65. lupine	108. purine	151. tub
23. brunet	66. lure	109. purl	152. tube
24. brunt	67. lute	110. put	153. tuber
25. brute	68. neb	111. reb	154. tulip
26. built	69. net	112. rebut	155. tun
27. bun	70. nib	113. rein	156. tune
28. bunt	71. nil	114. rent	157. tuner
29. bunter	72. nip	115. rep	158. Tupi
30. bur	73. nit	116. rib	159. turbine
31. buret	74. niter	117. riel	160. turn
32. burl	75. nitre	118. rile	161. turnip
33. burn	76. nub	119. rip	162. unit
34. burnt	77. nubile	120. ripe	163. unite
35. burp	78. nut	121. ripen	164. unripe
36. but	79. pelt	122. rite	165. untie
37. butler	80. pen	123. rub	166. until
38. erupt	81. pent	124. rube	167. urine
39. inept	82. per	125. ruble	168. urn
40. inert	83. peril	126. rue	169. Ute
41. inlet	84. pert	127. ruin	170. uteri
42. input	85. pet	128. rule	171. utile
43. inter	86. pie	129. run	

#18

How many words can you make from these 9 letters? There is no letter which must be used in every word. You can use only these 9 letters and a letter cannot be used more than once in any word (you may use 2 O's and 2 D's). It's possible to make one 9-letter word.

Score: 20 words or more – EXCELLENT

    15 words or more – VERY GOOD

    10 words or more – GOOD

Hint: don't forget the plural forms of words, for example hole is 1 word and holes is a 2ⁿᵈ word. It's possible to make 100 words of 3 or more letters. (See following page for answers).

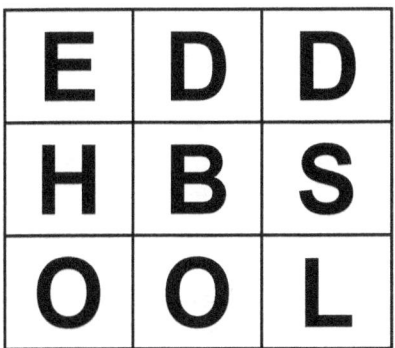

Your Answers:

1. bed	35. doles	69. lode
2. beds	36. doodle	70. lodes
3. behold	37. doodles	71. loose
4. beholds	38. dos	72. loosed
5. bled	39. dose	73. lose
6. blood	40. dosed	74. oboe
7. blooded	41. held	75. oboes
8. bloods	42. hob	76. odd
9. bloodshed	43. hobo	77. odds
10. bod	44. hoboed	78. ode
11. bode	45. hoboes	79. odes
12. boded	46. hobos	80. old
13. bodes	47. hobs	81. oleo
14. bods	48. hod	82. oleos
15. bold	49. hods	83. oodles
16. bole	50. hoe	84. she
17. boles	51. hoed	85. shed
18. bolo	52. hoes	86. shod
19. bolos	53. hold	87. shoe
20. boo	54. holds	88. shoo
21. boodle	55. hole	89. shooed
22. boodles	56. holed	90. sled
23. booed	57. holes	91. slob
24. boos	58. hood	92. sloe
25. bosh	59. hooded	93. sob
26. deb	60. hoods	94. sod
27. debs	61. hose	95. sol
28. dodo	62. hosed	96. sold
29. dodoes	63. led	97. sole
30. dodos	64. Leo	98. soled
31. doe	65. lob	99. solo
32. does	66. lobe	100. soloed
33. dole	67. lobes	
34. doled	68. lobs	

#19

How many words can you make from these 9 letters? Every word must contain the letter "E". You can use only these 9 letters and a letter cannot be used more than once in any word (you may use 2 S's). It's possible to make one 9-letter word.

Score: 20 words or more – EXCELLENT

    15 words or more – VERY GOOD

    10 words or more – GOOD

Hint: don't forget the plural forms of words, for example age is 1 word and ages is a 2nd word. It's possible to make 157 words of 3 or more letters. (See following page for answers).

Your Answers:

_____ _____ _____

_____ _____ _____ _____

_____ _____ _____ _____

_____ _____ _____ _____

_____ _____ _____ _____

_____ _____ _____ _____

_____ _____ _____ _____

_____ _____ _____ _____

_____ _____ _____ _____

_____ _____ _____ _____

_____ _____ _____ _____

1. able	41. blear	81. glues	121. saber
2. abler	42. blears	82. gruel	122. sabers
3. abuse	43. bless	83. guess	123. sable
4. abuser	44. blue	84. lager	124. sables
5. abuses	45. bluegrass	85. lagers	125. sabre
6. age	46. bluer	86. large	126. sabres
7. ager	47. blues	87. largess	127. sage
8. ages	48. bugle	88. laser	128. sager
9. ague	49. bugler	89. lasers	129. sages
10. agues	50. bugles	90. lea	130. sale
11. ale	51. bulge	91. leg	131. sales
12. ales	52. bulges	92. legs	132. sea
13. are	53. burgess	93. less	133. seal
14. Ares	54. burgle	94. leu	134. seals
15. argue	55. burgles	95. lube	135. sear
16. argues	56. bursae	96. lubes	136. sears
17. assure	57. buses	97. luge	137. seas
18. auger	58. ear	98. luger	138. sera
19. augers	59. earl	99. luges	139. Serb
20. bagel	60. earls	100. lure	140. Serbs
21. bagels	61. ears	101. lures	141. slue
22. bale	62. era	102. rage	142. slues
23. baler	63. erg	103. rages	143. sue
24. bales	64. ergs	104. rase	144. suer
25. bare	65. gable	105. rases	145. sues
26. bares	66. gables	106. real	146. sure
27. barge	67. Gael	107. reals	147. surge
28. barges	68. Gaels	108. reb	148. surges
29. base	69. gale	109. rebs	149. urea
30. baser	70. gales	110. rebus	150. urge
31. bases	71. garble	111. regal	151. urges
32. bear	72. garbles	112. rube	152. usable
33. bears	73. gases	113. rubes	153. usage
34. beau	74. gear	114. ruble	154. use
35. beaus	75. gears	115. rubles	155. user
36. beg	76. gel	116. rue	156. users
37. begs	77. gels	117. rues	157. uses
38. beluga	78. glare	118. rule	
39. blare	79. glares	119. rules	
40. blares	80. glue	120. ruse	

#20

How many words can you make from these 9 letters? There is no letter which must be used in every word. You can use only these 9 letters and a letter cannot be used more than once in any word. It's possible to make one 9-letter word.

Score: 20 words or more – EXCELLENT

     15 words or more – VERY GOOD

     10 words or more – GOOD

It's possible to make 199 words of 3 or more letters. (See following page for answers).

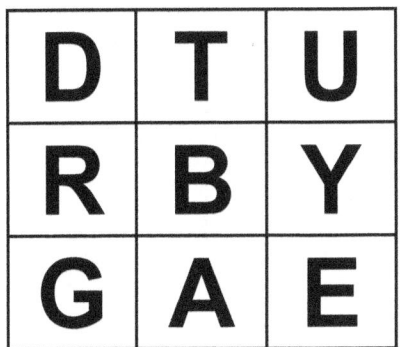

Your Answers:

1. abed	51. brat	101. eat	151. rub
2. abet	52. bray	102. edgy	152. rube
3. abut	53. brayed	103. era	153. ruby
4. aery	54. bread	104. erg	154. rude
5. age	55. bred	105. gab	155. rue
6. aged	56. brute	106. gad	156. rued
7. ager	57. bud	107. gar	157. rug
8. ague	58. budge	108. garb	158. rugby
9. are	59. budget	109. garbed	159. rut
10. argue	60. budgetary	110. gate	160. rye
11. argued	61. bug	111. gated	161. tab
12. art	62. bur	112. gater	162. tabu
13. arty	63. buret	113. gaudy	163. tabued
14. ate	64. burg	114. gay	164. tad
15. auger	65. bury	115. gayer	165. tag
16. aye	66. but	116. gear	166. tar
17. bad	67. buy	117. get	167. tardy
18. bade	68. bye	118. grab	168. tare
19. badge	69. byte	119. grad	169. tared
20. badger	70. dab	120. grade	170. tau
21. bag	71. dag	121. grate	171. tea
22. bar	72. dare	122. grated	172. tear
23. bard	73. dart	123. gray	173. teary
24. bare	74. date	124. grayed	174. trade
25. bared	75. dater	125. great	175. tragedy
26. barge	76. daub	126. grey	176. tray
27. barged	77. dauber	127. grub	177. tread
28. bat	78. daubery	128. guar	178. trey
29. bate	79. day	129. guard	179. trudge
30. bated	80. dear	130. gut	180. true
31. baud	81. deb	131. guy	181. trued
32. bay	82. debar	132. guyed	182. try
33. bayed	83. debt	133. gybe	183. Tuareg
34. bead	84. debug	134. gybed	184. tub
35. beady	85. debut	135. gyrate	185. tuba
36. bear	86. derby	136. gyrated	186. tube
37. beard	87. drab	137. rad	187. tubed
38. beat	88. drag	138. rag	188. tuber
39. beau	89. dray	139. rage	189. tug
40. beaut	90. drub	140. raged	190. tyre
41. beauty	91. drug	141. rat	191. urea
42. bed	92. dry	142. rate	192. urge
43. beg	93. dub	143. rated	193. urged
44. bet	94. due	144. ray	194. Ute
45. beta	95. duet	145. rayed	195. yard
46. betray	96. dug	146. read	196. yea
47. bey	97. duty	147. ready	197. year
48. bra	98. dye	148. reb	198. yet
49. brad	99. dyer	149. rebut	199. yurt
50. brag	100. ear	150. red	

#21

How many words can you make from these 9 letters? There is no letter which must be used in every word. You can use only these 9 letters and a letter cannot be used more than once in any word (you may use 2 A's). It's possible to make one 9-letter word.

Score: 20 words or more – EXCELLENT

15 words or more – VERY GOOD

10 words or more – GOOD

It's possible to make 135 words of 3 or more letters. (See following page for answers).

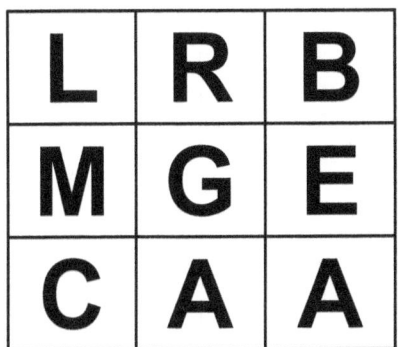

Your Answers:

1. abeam	35. baler	69. clam	103. gram
2. able	36. balm	70. clamber	104. lab
3. abler	37. bar	71. clear	105. lace
4. ace	38. bare	72. crab	106. lacer
5. acerb	39. barge	73. crag	107. lag
6. acme	40. beam	74. cram	108. lager
7. acre	41. bear	75. cream	109. lam
8. agar	42. becalm	76. ear	110. lama
9. age	43. beg	77. earl	111. lamb
10. ager	44. berm	78. elm	112. lame
11. agleam	45. blame	79. era	113. lamer
12. ala	46. blamer	80. erg	114. large
13. alae	47. blare	81. gab	115. lea
14. alarm	48. blear	82. gable	116. leg
15. alb	49. bra	83. Gaea	117. macabre
16. ale	50. brace	84. Gael	118. mace
17. alga	51. brag	85. gal	119. male
18. algae	52. bream	86. gala	120. mar
19. algebra	53. cab	87. gale	121. marble
20. amber	54. cabal	88. gamble	122. mare
21. amble	55. cable	89. gambler	123. marl
22. ambler	56. cablegram	90. game	124. meal
23. ameba	57. cabler	91. gamer	125. race
24. Arab	58. cage	92. gar	126. rag
25. arable	59. calm	93. garb	127. rage
26. arc	60. calmer	94. garble	128. ram
27. are	61. cam	95. gear	129. Rama
28. area	62. camber	96. gel	130. ramble
29. arm	63. came	97. gem	131. real
30. baa	64. camel	98. germ	132. realm
31. Baal	65. camera	99. glare	133. ream
32. bag	66. car	100. gleam	134. reb
33. bagel	67. caramel	101. grab	135. regal
34. bale	68. care	102. grace	

#22

How many words can you make from these 9 letters? There is no letter which must be used in every word. You can use only these 9 letters and a letter cannot be used more than once in any word (you may use 2 A's and 2 E's). It's possible to make one 9-letter word.

Score: 20 words or more – EXCELLENT

    15 words or more – VERY GOOD

    10 words or more – GOOD

It's possible to make 93 words of 3 or more letters. (See following page for answers).

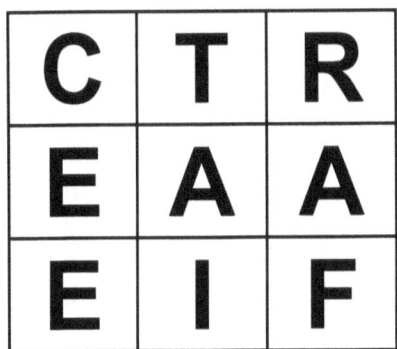

Your Answers:

1. ace	32. create	63. free
2. acre	33. Cree	64. fret
3. act	34. ear	65. ice
4. aerate	35. eat	66. irate
5. aerie	36. eater	67. ire
6. afar	37. era	68. race
7. afire	38. ere	69. raft
8. aft	39. erect	70. rat
9. after	40. Erie	71. rate
10. air	41. face	72. react
11. arc	42. facet	73. recite
12. are	43. fact	74. recta
13. area	44. faerie	75. reef
14. aria	45. fair	76. rice
15. art	46. far	77. rife
16. ate	47. farce	78. rift
17. atria	48. fare	79. rite
18. cafe	49. fat	80. Tai
19. cafeteria	50. fate	81. tar
20. car	51. fear	82. tare
21. carafe	52. feat	83. tea
22. carat	53. fee	84. tear
23. care	54. feet	85. tee
24. caret	55. feta	86. tiara
25. cart	56. fete	87. tic
26. cat	57. fiat	88. tie
27. cater	58. fie	89. tier
28. cir	59. fierce	90. tire
29. cite	60. fir	91. trace
30. craft	61. fire	92. tree
31. crate	62. fit	93. trice

#23

How many words can you make from these 9 letters? Every word must contain the letter "E". You can use only these 9 letters and a letter cannot be used more than once in any word (you may use 2 A's). It's possible to make one 9-letter word.

Score: 20 words or more – EXCELLENT

    15 words or more – VERY GOOD

    10 words or more – GOOD

Hint: don't forget the plural forms of words, for example earn is 1 word and earns is a 2nd word. It's possible to make 147 words of 4 or more letters. (See following page for answers).

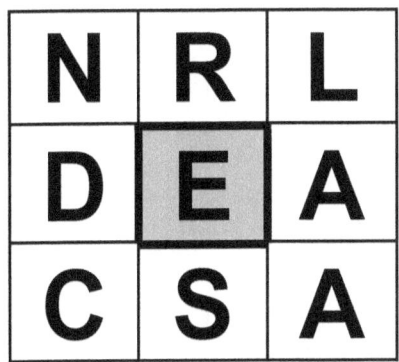

Your Answers:

1. aced	38. canes	75. earls	112. nerd
2. aces	39. care	76. earn	113. nerds
3. acne	40. cared	77. earns	114. race
4. acre	41. cares	78. ears	115. raced
5. acres	42. case	79. eland	116. races
6. adrenal	43. cased	80. elands	117. rase
7. adrenals	44. cedar	81. ends	118. rased
8. alae	45. cedars	82. lace	119. read
9. alder	46. clean	83. laced	120. reads
10. alders	47. cleans	84. lacer	121. real
11. ales	48. clear	85. laces	122. reals
12. arcade	49. clears	86. lade	123. reds
13. arcades	50. cradle	87. laden	124. renal
14. arcane	51. cradles	88. lades	125. rend
15. arced	52. crane	89. lance	126. rends
16. area	53. craned	90. lanced	127. sacred
17. areas	54. cranes	91. lancer	128. sale
18. arena	55. dace	92. lancers	129. sander
19. arenas	56. daces	93. lances	130. sane
20. Ares	57. dale	94. lane	131. saner
21. arsenal	58. dales	95. lanes	132. Saracen
22. ascend	59. dance	96. laser	133. scale
23. cadre	60. dancer	97. lead	134. scaled
24. Caesar	61. dances	98. leads	135. scare
25. caldera	62. Dane	99. lean	136. scared
26. calendar	63. Danes	100. leans	137. sclera
27. calendars	64. dare	101. learn	138. seal
28. calends	65. dares	102. learns	139. sear
29. canaled	66. deal	103. lend	140. sedan
30. candela	67. deals	104. lends	141. send
31. candelas	68. dean	105. lens	142. sera
32. candle	69. deans	106. nacre	143. slander
33. candler	70. dear	107. nacred	144. sled
34. candles	71. dears	108. nacres	145. snare
35. cane	72. decal	109. nares	146. snared
36. caned	73. dens	110. near	147. snarled
37. caner	74. earl	111. nears	

#24

How many words can you make from these 9 letters? There is no letter which must be used in every word. You can use only these 9 letters and a letter cannot be used more than once in any word (you may use 2 A's). It's possible to make one 9-letter word.

Score: 20 words or more – EXCELLENT

     15 words or more – VERY GOOD

     10 words or more – GOOD

It's possible to make 176 words of 3 or more letters. (See following page for answers).

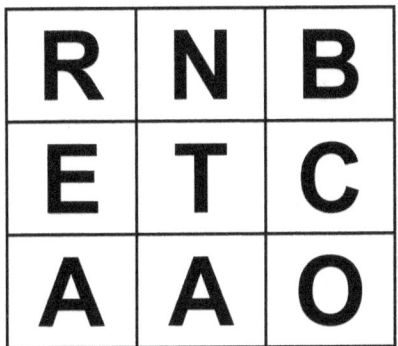

Your Answers:

1. abate	45. beat	89. cero	133. orb
2. abet	46. bent	90. coat	134. orca
3. abort	47. bet	91. cob	135. ore
4. ace	48. beta	92. cobra	136. ornate
5. acerb	49. boa	93. con	137. race
6. acne	50. boar	94. cone	138. ran
7. acorn	51. boat	95. core	139. rant
8. acre	52. boater	96. corn	140. rat
9. acrobat	53. Boer	97. cornea	141. rate
10. act	54. bone	98. cornet	142. react
11. actor	55. boner	99. cot	143. reb
12. aeon	56. borate	100. cote	144. recant
13. aerobat	57. bore	101. crab	145. recta
14. ant	58. born	102. crane	146. recto
15. ante	59. borne	103. crate	147. rent
16. aorta	60. bra	104. Croat	148. roan
17. aortae	61. brace	105. crone	149. rob
18. Arab	62. bract	106. ear	150. robe
19. arc	63. bran	107. earn	151. roe
20. arcane	64. brant	108. eat	152. rot
21. are	65. brat	109. enact	153. rote
22. area	66. Breton	110. enactor	154. tab
23. arena	67. cab	111. eon	155. tabor
24. art	68. cabaret	112. era	156. taco
25. ate	69. can	113. nab	157. tan
26. atone	70. cane	114. nacre	158. tar
27. atoner	71. caner	115. nae	159. tare
28. baa	72. canoe	116. narc	160. tarn
29. bacon	73. cant	117. near	161. taro
30. ban	74. canter	118. neat	162. tea
31. bane	75. canto	119. neb	163. tear
32. banter	76. cantor	120. nectar	164. ten
33. bar	77. car	121. net	165. tenor
34. bare	78. carat	122. nor	166. tern
35. barn	79. carbon	123. not	167. toe
36. baron	80. carbonate	124. note	168. toea
37. baronet	81. care	125. noter	169. ton
38. bat	82. caret	126. oar	170. tone
39. bate	83. carob	127. oat	171. toner
40. baton	84. cart	128. ocean	172. tor
41. beacon	85. carton	129. octane	173. tore
42. bean	86. cat	130. once	174. torn
43. beano	87. cater	131. one	175. trace
44. bear	88. cent	132. orate	176. trance

car·bon·ate (kär′bə-nāt′) *tr.v.* **car·bon·at·ed, car·bon·at·ing, car·bon·ates. 1.** To charge (a beverage, for example) with carbon dioxide gas. **2.** To burn to carbon; carbonize. **3.** To change into a carbonate. **--car·bon·ate** (-nāt′, -nĭt) *n.* A salt or ester of carbonic acid. **--car′bon·a′tion** *n.* **--car′bon·a′tor** *n.*

#25

How many words can you make from these 9 letters? There is no letter which must be used in every word. You can use only these 9 letters and a letter cannot be used more than once in any word (you may use 2 E's). It's possible to make one 9-letter word.

Score: 20 words or more – EXCELLENT

    15 words or more – VERY GOOD

    10 words or more – GOOD

It's possible to make 162 words of 3 or more letters. (See following page for answers).

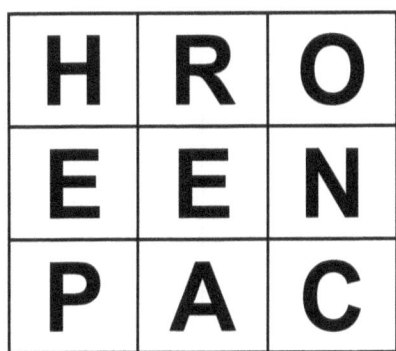

H	R	O
E	E	N
P	A	C

Your Answers:

1. ace	42. chorea	83. heron	124. peahen
2. ache	43. cohere	84. hoe	125. pean
3. achene	44. con	85. hoer	126. pear
4. acne	45. cone	86. hone	127. pecan
5. acorn	46. cop	87. hop	128. peen
6. acre	47. cope	88. hope	129. peer
7. aeon	48. coper	89. hoper	130. pen
8. anchor	49. copra	90. horn	131. pence
9. ape	50. core	91. nacho	132. peon
10. aper	51. corn	92. nacre	133. per
11. apron	52. cornea	93. nae	134. perch
12. arc	53. crane	94. nap	135. phone
13. arch	54. crape	95. nape	136. poach
14. are	55. Cree	96. narc	137. poacher
15. can	56. creep	97. near	138. pone
16. cane	57. crepe	98. nee	139. porch
17. caner	58. crone	99. Noh	140. pore
18. canoe	59. crop	100. nope	141. porn
19. cap	60. each	101. nor	142. prance
20. cape	61. ear	102. oar	143. preach
21. caper	62. earn	103. ocean	144. preen
22. capo	63. earphone	104. ocher	145. pro
23. capon	64. echo	105. ochre	146. prone
24. car	65. echoer	106. once	147. race
25. care	66. encore	107. one	148. ran
26. careen	67. eon	108. open	149. ranch
27. carhop	68. epoch	109. opera	150. ranee
28. carp	69. era	110. orca	151. rap
29. cero	70. ere	111. ore	152. rape
30. chap	71. hap	112. orphan	153. reach
31. chaperon	72. hare	113. pace	154. reap
32. chaperone	73. harp	114. pacer	155. recap
33. char	74. heap	115. pan	156. rep
34. cheap	75. hear	116. pane	157. rhea
35. cheapen	76. hen	117. panoche	158. rho
36. cheaper	77. hence	118. par	159. roach
37. cheep	78. her	119. parch	160. roan
38. cheer	79. Hera	120. pare	161. roe
39. chon	80. here	121. pea	162. rope
40. chop	81. hereon	122. peace	
41. chore	82. hero	123. peach	

#26

How many words can you make from these 9 letters? There is no letter which must be used in every word. You can use only these 9 letters and a letter cannot be used more than once in any word. It's possible to make one 9-letter word.

Score: 20 words or more – EXCELLENT

15 words or more – VERY GOOD

10 words or more – GOOD

Hint: don't forget the plural forms of words, for example chin is 1 word and chins is a 2nd word. It's possible to make 111 words of 3 or more letters. (See following page for answers).

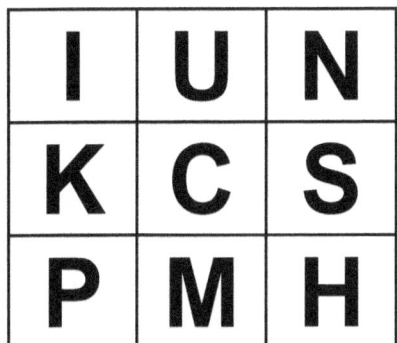

I	U	N
K	C	S
P	M	H

Your Answers:

1. chi	38. imps	75. Punic
2. chimp	39. inch	76. punish
3. chimps	40. incus	77. punk
4. chin	41. ink	78. punks
5. chink	42. inks	79. puns
6. chinks	43. ins	80. pus
7. chins	44. kin	81. push
8. chip	45. kip	82. scum
9. chipmunk	46. knish	83. shim
10. chipmunks	47. min	84. shin
11. chips	48. mink	85. ship
12. chum	49. minks	86. shmuck
13. chump	50. minus	87. shuck
14. chumps	51. much	88. shun
15. chums	52. muck	89. sic
16. chunk	53. mucks	90. sick
17. chunks	54. munch	91. Sikh
18. cumin	55. mush	92. sin
19. cup	56. music	93. sink
20. cups	57. musk	94. sip
21. cusp	58. nick	95. ski
22. hick	59. nicks	96. skim
23. hicks	60. nip	97. skimp
24. him	61. nips	98. skin
25. hip	62. phi	99. skip
26. hips	63. pick	100. snip
27. his	64. picks	101. snuck
28. hum	65. pin	102. spin
29. hump	66. pinch	103. spun
30. humps	67. pink	104. spunk
31. hums	68. pinks	105. such
32. Hun	69. pins	106. suck
33. hunk	70. puck	107. sum
34. hunks	71. puckish	108. sump
35. Huns	72. pucks	109. sun
36. husk	73. pun	110. sunk
37. imp	74. punch	111. sup

#27

How many words can you make from these 9 letters? There is no letter which must be used in every word. You can use only these 9 letters and a letter cannot be used more than once in any word (you may use 2 I's). It's possible to make one 9-letter word.

Score: 20 words or more – EXCELLENT

    15 words or more – VERY GOOD

    10 words or more – GOOD

Hint: don't forget the plural forms of words, for example chin is 1 word and chins is a 2nd word. It's possible to make 118 words of 3 or more letters. (See following page for answers).

Your Answers: _____ _____ _____

_____ _____ _____ _____

_____ _____ _____ _____

_____ _____ _____ _____

_____ _____ _____ _____

_____ _____ _____ _____

_____ _____ _____ _____

_____ _____ _____ _____

_____ _____ _____ _____

_____ _____ _____ _____

_____ _____ _____ _____

1. chi	41. huts	81. Sion
2. chin	42. icon	82. sit
3. chino	43. icons	83. snit
4. chinos	44. ictus	84. snitch
5. chins	45. inch	85. snot
6. chit	46. incus	86. snout
7. chitin	47. ins	87. son
8. chitinous	48. inti	88. sonic
9. chiton	49. intis	89. sot
10. chits	50. into	90. south
11. chon	51. Inuit	91. stoic
12. cion	52. Inuits	92. stun
13. coin	53. ion	93. such
14. coins	54. itch	94. suction
15. coitus	55. its	95. suit
16. con	56. nit	96. sun
17. cons	57. nits	97. thin
18. cost	58. Noh	98. thins
19. cot	59. nosh	99. this
20. cots	60. not	100.thou
21. count	61. notch	101.thus
22. counts	62. nut	102.tic
23. cousin	63. nuts	103.tics
24. cushion	64. onus	104.tin
25. cut	65. ouch	105.tins
26. cuts	66. oust	106.tis
27. hint	67. out	107.tocsin
28. hints	68. outs	108.ton
29. his	69. scion	109.tonic
30. hit	70. Scot	110.tonics
31. hits	71. scout	111.tons
32. hoist	72. shin	112.touch
33. host	73. Shinto	113.tun
34. hot	74. shot	114.tunic
35. hots	75. shout	115.tuns
36. Hun	76. shun	116.unit
37. Huns	77. shunt	117.units
38. hunt	78. shut	118.unto
39. hunts	79. sic	
40. hut	80. sin	

chi·tin (kīt′n) *n.* A tough, protective, semitransparent substance, primarily a nitrogen-containing polysaccharide, forming the principal component of arthropod exoskeletons and the cell walls of certain fungi. **--chi′tin·ous** *adj.*

54

#28

How many words can you make from these 9 letters? Every word must contain the letter "E". You can use only these 9 letters and a letter cannot be used more than once in any word. It's possible to make one 9-letter word.

Score: 20 words or more – EXCELLENT

    15 words or more – VERY GOOD

    10 words or more – GOOD

Hint: don't forget the plural forms of words, for example code is 1 word and codes is a 2nd word. It's possible to make 171 words of 4 or more letters. (See following page for answers).

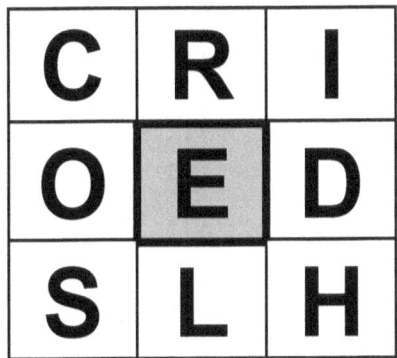

Your Answers:

1. cedi	44. dices	87. iced	130. riled
2. cedis	45. dies	88. ices	131. riles
3. cero	46. dire	89. ides	132. rise
4. ceros	47. docile	90. idle	133. rode
5. chide	48. doer	91. idler	134. roes
6. chider	49. doers	92. idles	135. roiled
7. chides	50. does	93. isle	136. role
8. chisel	51. dole	94. leis	137. roles
9. chloride	52. doles	95. lice	138. rose
10. chlorides	53. dories	96. lied	139. scolder
11. choired	54. dose	97. lies	140. score
12. choler	55. doser	98. lire	141. scored
13. chore	56. dries	99. lode	142. shed
14. chores	57. echo	100. lodes	143. sherd
15. chose	58. Eros	101. lore	144. shied
16. cider	59. heir	102. lose	145. shield
17. ciders	60. heirs	103. ocher	146. shier
18. close	61. held	104. ochre	147. shire
19. closed	62. herd	105. ochres	148. shoe
20. closer	63. herds	106. odes	149. shore
21. code	64. hero	107. oiled	150. shored
22. codes	65. heroic	108. oiler	151. shred
23. coed	66. heroics	109. oilers	152. side
24. coeds	67. hers	110. older	153. sidle
25. coiled	68. hide	111. oldie	154. siloed
26. coiler	69. hides	112. oldies	155. sire
27. colder	70. hied	113. oriel	156. sired
28. core	71. hies	114. osier	157. sled
29. cored	72. hire	115. reds	158. slice
30. cores	73. hired	116. reis	159. sliced
31. cosied	74. hires	117. relic	160. slicer
32. cosier	75. hoed	118. relics	161. slide
33. credo	76. hoer	119. relish	162. slider
34. credos	77. hoes	120. resh	163. slier
35. cried	78. hole	121. rice	164. sloe
36. cries	79. holed	122. riced	165. soiled
37. decor	80. holes	123. rices	166. solder
38. decors	81. holier	124. riches	167. soldier
39. deli	82. horde	125. ride	168. sole
40. delis	83. horse	126. rides	169. soled
41. dice	84. horsed	127. riel	170. solider
42. dicer	85. hose	128. riels	171. sore
43. dicers	86. hosed	129. rile	

#29

How many words can you make from these 9 letters? There is no letter which must be used in every word. You can use only these 9 letters and a letter cannot be used more than once in any word. It's possible to make one 9-letter word.

Score: 20 words or more – EXCELLENT

    15 words or more – VERY GOOD

    10 words or more – GOOD

It's possible to make 167 words of 3 or more letters. (See following page for answers).

E	A	R
M	C	G
Y	N	L

Your Answers:

1. ace	43. clear	85. gym	127. mean
2. acme	44. clergy	86. lac	128. meanly
3. acne	45. clergyman	87. lace	129. men
4. acre	46. crag	88. lacer	130. mercy
5. aery	47. cram	89. lag	131. myna
6. age	48. crane	90. lager	132. nacre
7. agency	49. cream	91. lam	133. nae
8. ager	50. cry	92. lame	134. nag
9. ale	51. cyan	93. lamer	135. name
10. amen	52. ear	94. lance	136. namely
11. angel	53. earl	95. lancer	137. namer
12. anger	54. early	96. lane	138. narc
13. angle	55. earn	97. larceny	139. nary
14. angry	56. elm	98. large	140. nay
15. any	57. era	99. lay	141. near
16. arc	58. erg	100. layer	142. nearly
17. are	59. Gael	101. laymen	143. race
18. argyle	60. gal	102. lea	144. racy
19. arm	61. gale	103. lean	145. rag
20. army	62. game	104. learn	146. rage
21. aye	63. gamely	105. leg	147. ram
22. cage	64. gamer	106. legacy	148. ran
23. cagey	65. gamey	107. ley	149. rang
24. cagy	66. gamy	108. lye	150. range
25. calm	67. gar	109. Lyra	151. rangy
26. calmer	68. gay	110. lyre	152. ray
27. cam	69. gayer	111. mace	153. real
28. came	70. gear	112. male	154. realm
29. camel	71. gel	113. man	155. ream
30. can	72. gem	114. mane	156. regal
31. cane	73. germ	115. mange	157. relay
32. caner	74. German	116. manger	158. rely
33. car	75. glance	117. mangle	159. renal
34. care	76. glare	118. mangler	160. rye
35. carney	77. gleam	119. manly	161. yam
36. carny	78. glean	120. many	162. yang
37. cay	79. glen	121. mar	163. yarn
38. clam	80. gnarl	122. mare	164. yea
39. clan	81. grace	123. marl	165. year
40. clang	82. gram	124. marly	166. yearn
41. clay	83. gray	125. may	167. yen
42. clean	84. grey	126. meal	

#30

How many words can you make from these 9 letters? Every word must contain the letter "E". You can use only these 9 letters and a letter cannot be used more than once in any word. It's possible to make one 9-letter word.

Score: 20 words or more – EXCELLENT

    15 words or more – VERY GOOD

    10 words or more – GOOD

Hint: don't forget the plural forms of words, for example edit is 1 word and edits is a 2nd word. It's possible to make 140 words of 4 or more letters. (See following page for answers).

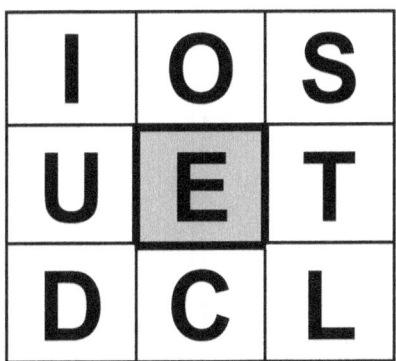

Your Answers:

1. cedi	36. diet	71. lets	106. slide
2. cedis	37. diets	72. lice	107. sloe
3. Celt	38. dilute	73. lied	108. slue
4. Celts	39. dilutes	74. lies	109. slued
5. cite	40. docile	75. lieu	110. sluice
6. cited	41. does	76. listed	111. sluiced
7. cites	42. dole	77. lode	112. soiled
8. close	43. doles	78. lodes	113. sole
9. closed	44. dose	79. lose	114. soled
10. closet	45. dote	80. loudest	115. solitude
11. cloudiest	46. dotes	81. louse	116. solute
12. clouted	47. douse	82. loused	117. stile
13. clue	48. ductile	83. Lucite	118. stole
14. clued	49. duel	84. lusted	119. sued
15. clues	50. duelist	85. lute	120. suet
16. code	51. duels	86. lutes	121. suite
17. codes	52. dues	87. odes	122. suited
18. coed	53. duet	88. oiled	123. tedious
19. coeds	54. dulcet	89. oldest	124. tide
20. coiled	55. duties	90. oldie	125. tides
21. coldest	56. edict	91. oldies	126. tied
22. coleus	57. edicts	92. ousted	127. ties
23. cosied	58. edit	93. outed	128. tilde
24. cote	59. edits	94. outside	129. tildes
25. cotes	60. escudo	95. scouted	130. tile
26. cued	61. iced	96. sect	131. tiled
27. cues	62. ices	97. side	132. tiles
28. cute	63. ides	98. sidle	133. toed
29. deist	64. idle	99. siloed	134. toes
30. deli	65. idles	100. silted	135. toiled
31. delis	66. idlest	101. site	136. tousle
32. deltic	67. isle	102. sited	137. tousled
33. dice	68. islet	103. sled	138. used
34. dices	69. leis	104. slice	139. Utes
35. dies	70. lest	105. sliced	140. utile

#31

How many words can you make from these 9 letters? There is no letter which must be used in every word. You can use only these 9 letters and a letter cannot be used more than once in any word (you may use 2 N's). It's possible to make one 9-letter word.

Score: 20 words or more – EXCELLENT

    15 words or more – VERY GOOD

    10 words or more – GOOD

It's possible to make 135 words of 3 or more letters. (See following page for answers).

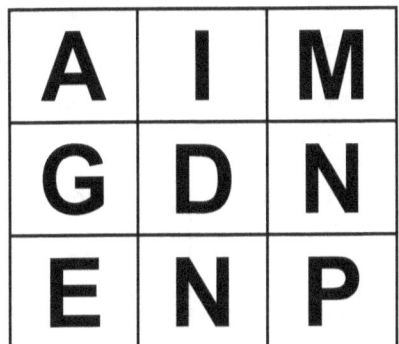

Your Answers:

1. age	35. dime	69. mad	103. nape
2. aged	36. din	70. made	104. nine
3. aid	37. dine	71. magi	105. nip
4. aide	38. ding	72. magpie	106. pad
5. aim	39. dip	73. maid	107. page
6. aimed	40. Edam	74. maiden	108. paged
7. amen	41. end	75. main	109. paid
8. amend	42. ending	76. man	110. pain
9. amending	43. enigma	77. mane	111. pained
10. amid	44. gad	78. mange	112. pan
11. amine	45. gain	79. manned	113. pane
12. amp	46. gained	80. map	114. pang
13. and	47. game	81. mead	115. panged
14. ape	48. gamed	82. mean	116. panned
15. aped	49. gamin	83. meaning	117. pea
16. aping	50. gamine	84. media	118. pean
17. dag	51. gap	85. median	119. peg
18. Dai	52. gape	86. men	120. pen
19. dam	53. gaped	87. mend	121. pending
20. dame	54. gem	88. mending	122. penman
21. damn	55. gimp	89. mid	123. penni
22. damning	56. gimped	90. midge	124. pennia
23. damp	57. gin	91. mien	125. pie
24. dampen	58. ginned	92. min	126. pied
25. dampening	59. gip	93. mina	127. pig
26. damping	60. idea	94. mind	128. Pima
27. Dane	61. idem	95. mine	129. Piman
28. dean	62. image	96. mined	130. pin
29. deign	63. imaged	97. nae	131. pine
30. den	64. imp	98. nag	132. pined
31. denim	65. imped	99. name	133. ping
32. die	66. impend	100. named	134. pinged
33. dig	67. inane	101. naming	135. pinned
34. dim	68. inn	102. nap	

#32

How many words can you make from these 9 letters?
There is no letter which must be used in every word.
You can use only these 9 letters and a letter cannot be
used more than once in any word (you may use 2 D's
and 2 N's). It's possible to make one 9-letter word.
Score: 20 words or more – EXCELLENT
      15 words or more – VERY GOOD
      10 words or more – GOOD
It's possible to make 121 words of 3 or more letters.
(See following page for answers).

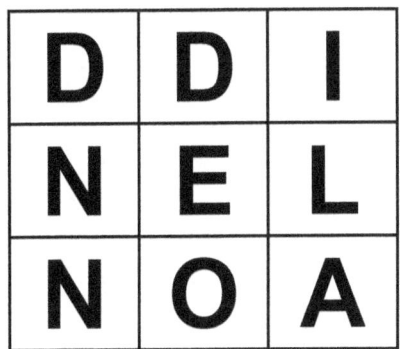

Your Answers:

1. add	42. died	83. lend
2. addle	43. din	84. Leo
3. adenoid	44. dine	85. liane
4. ado	45. dined	86. lid
5. aeon	46. dinned	87. lie
6. aid	47. diode	88. lied
7. aide	48. doe	89. lien
8. aided	49. dole	90. linden
9. ail	50. doled	91. line
10. ailed	51. don	92. lined
11. ale	52. done	93. linen
12. alien	53. donned	94. lion
13. aline	54. eland	95. load
14. alined	55. end	96. loaded
15. aloe	56. eolian	97. loan
16. alone	57. eon	98. loaned
17. and	58. idea	99. lode
18. anion	59. ideal	100. loin
19. annelid	60. idle	101. lone
20. anode	61. idled	102. nae
21. anole	62. idol	103. nail
22. anon	63. ilea	104. nailed
23. dad	64. inane	105. neon
24. dado	65. inland	106. nil
25. Dai	66. inn	107. nine
26. dal	67. ion	108. nod
27. dale	68. lad	109. node
28. dandelion	69. lade	110. noel
29. dandle	70. laded	111. none
30. Dane	71. laden	112. odd
31. dead	72. ladino	113. ode
32. deal	73. laid	114. Odin
33. dean	74. lain	115. oil
34. deli	75. land	116. oiled
35. den	76. landed	117. old
36. denial	77. lane	118. olden
37. dial	78. lea	119. oldie
38. dialed	79. lead	120. one
39. did	80. lean	121. Oneida
40. dido	81. led	
41. die	82. lei	

#33

How many words can you make from these 9 letters? There is no letter which must be used in every word. You can use only these 9 letters and a letter cannot be used more than once in any word (you may use 2 D's and 2 A's). It's possible to make one 9-letter word.

Score: 20 words or more – EXCELLENT

15 words or more – VERY GOOD

10 words or more – GOOD

Hint: don't forget the plural forms of words, for example add is 1 word and adds is a 2nd word. It's possible to make 117 words of 3 or more letters. (See following page for answers).

A	M	Y
A	E	S
D	D	R

Your Answers: _____ _____ _____

_____ _____ _____

_____ _____ _____

_____ _____ _____

_____ _____ _____

_____ _____ _____

_____ _____ _____

_____ _____ _____

_____ _____ _____

_____ _____ _____

_____ _____ _____

1.	add	40.	drams
2.	adder	41.	dray
3.	adders	42.	drayed
4.	adds	43.	drays
5.	ads	44.	dread
6.	aery	45.	dreads
7.	are	46.	dream
8.	area	47.	dreams
9.	areas	48.	dry
10.	Ares	49.	dryad
11.	arm	50.	drys
12.	armed	51.	dye
13.	arms	52.	dyed
14.	army	53.	dyer
15.	aye	54.	dyes
16.	ayes	55.	ear
17.	dad	56.	ears
18.	dada	57.	easy
19.	dadas	58.	Edam
20.	dads	59.	eddy
21.	dam	60.	era
22.	dame	61.	mad
23.	dames	62.	madder
24.	dams	63.	madders
25.	dare	64.	made
26.	dared	65.	madras
27.	dares	66.	mads
28.	daresay	67.	mar
29.	day	68.	mare
30.	daydream	69.	mares
31.	daydreams	70.	mars
32.	days	71.	maser
33.	dead	72.	may
34.	dear	73.	Maya
35.	dears	74.	Mayas
36.	derma	75.	mead
37.	dermas	76.	mesa
38.	dram	77.	rad
39.	drama	78.	rads

79.	ram
80.	Rama
81.	rams
82.	rase
83.	rased
84.	ray
85.	rayed
86.	rays
87.	read
88.	reads
89.	ready
90.	ream
91.	reams
92.	red
93.	reds
94.	rye
95.	ryes
96.	sad
97.	sadder
98.	same
99.	say
100.	sayer
101.	sea
102.	seam
103.	seamy
104.	sear
105.	sera
106.	smear
107.	smeary
108.	yam
109.	yams
110.	yard
111.	yarded
112.	yards
113.	yea
114.	year
115.	years
116.	yeas
117.	yes

#34

How many words can you make from these 9 letters? Every word must contain the letter "E". You can use only these 9 letters and a letter cannot be used more than once in any word. It's possible to make two 9-letter words.

Score: 20 words or more – EXCELLENT

15 words or more – VERY GOOD

10 words or more – GOOD

It's possible to make 138 words of 4 or more letters. (See following page for answers).

Your Answers:

1. aeon	36. dilate	71. flied	106. loaned
2. afield	37. dine	72. floated	107. lode
3. aide	38. dole	73. floe	108. lofted
4. ailed	39. donate	74. foaled	109. lone
5. alien	40. done	75. foetal	110. nailed
6. aline	41. dote	76. foetid	111. neat
7. alined	42. edit	77. foiled	112. node
8. aloe	43. eland	78. fondle	113. noel
9. alone	44. elation	79. idea	114. note
10. anode	45. enfold	80. ideal	115. noted
11. anole	46. entail	81. idle	116. often
12. ante	47. eolian	82. ilea	117. oiled
13. anted	48. fade	83. inflate	118. olden
14. atone	49. failed	84. inflated	119. oldie
15. atoned	50. fainted	85. inlet	120. Oneida
16. dale	51. fate	86. lade	121. tailed
17. Dane	52. fated	87. laden	122. tale
18. date	53. feat	88. lane	123. teal
19. deaf	54. feint	89. late	124. Teflon
20. deal	55. felon	90. lead	125. tend
21. dealt	56. felt	91. leaf	126. tide
22. dean	57. fend	92. lean	127. tied
23. defiant	58. feta	93. left	128. tilde
24. deflation	59. fetal	94. lend	129. tile
25. defoliant	60. fetid	95. lent	130. tiled
26. deft	61. field	96. lento	131. tine
27. delft	62. fiend	97. liane	132. tined
28. deli	63. file	98. lied	133. toea
29. delta	64. filed	99. lief	134. toed
30. denial	65. filet	100. lien	135. toenail
31. dent	66. finale	101. life	136. toiled
32. dental	67. fine	102. lifted	137. tone
33. detail	68. fined	103. line	138. toned
34. detain	69. flea	104. lined	
35. diet	70. fled	105. loafed	

#35

How many words can you make from these 9 letters? Every word must contain the letter "A". You can use only these 9 letters and a letter cannot be used more than once in any word. It's possible to make two 9-letter words.

Score: 20 words or more – EXCELLENT

    15 words or more – VERY GOOD

    10 words or more – GOOD

It's possible to make 180 words of 4 or more letters. (See following page for answers).

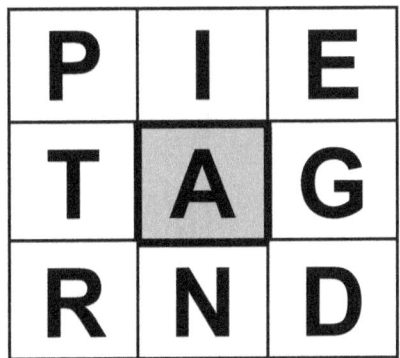

Your Answers:

1. adept	46. gainer	91. pair	136. rant
2. aged	47. gait	92. paired	137. ranted
3. agent	48. gaited	93. pander	138. rape
4. ager	49. gaiter	94. pane	139. raped
5. aide	50. gander	95. pang	140. rapid
6. aider	51. gape	96. panged	141. rapine
7. aigret	52. gaped	97. pant	142. raping
8. aired	53. garden	98. panted	143. rapt
9. anger	54. garnet	99. pantie	144. rate
10. ante	55. gate	100. pare	145. rated
11. anted	56. gated	101. pared	146. rating
12. anti	57. gear	102. parent	147. read
13. aped	58. giant	103. paring	148. reading
14. aping	59. gnat	104. part	149. reap
15. ardent	60. grad	105. parted	150. reaping
16. argent	61. grade	106. partied	151. regain
17. arid	62. gradient	107. parting	152. repaid
18. Dane	63. grain	108. pate	153. retain
19. danger	64. grained	109. pated	154. retina
20. dare	65. grand	110. paten	155. tang
21. daring	66. granite	111. patin	156. tanged
22. darn	67. grant	112. patine	157. tape
23. dart	68. granted	113. pean	158. taped
24. darting	69. grape	114. pear	159. taper
25. date	70. grate	115. peat	160. tapering
26. dater	71. grated	116. pedant	161. taping
27. dating	72. great	117. pertain	162. tapir
28. dean	73. idea	118. petard	163. tare
29. dear	74. inapt	119. pirate	164. tared
30. depart	75. ingrate	120. pirated	165. taring
31. departing	76. irate	121. pita	166. tarn
32. detain	77. nadir	122. prate	167. tarp
33. detrain	78. nape	123. prated	168. tear
34. diaper	79. nard	124. prating	169. tearing
35. dinar	80. near	125. predating	170. tirade
36. drag	81. neat	126. rage	171. trade
37. dragnet	82. padre	127. raged	172. trading
38. drain	83. page	128. raid	173. train
39. drape	84. paged	129. rain	174. trained
40. draping	85. paid	130. rained	175. trap
41. earn	86. pain	131. rand	176. tread
42. eating	87. pained	132. rang	177. treading
43. entrap	88. paint	133. range	178. trepan
44. gain	89. painted	134. ranged	179. triad
45. gained	90. painter	135. rani	180. triage

#36

How many words can you make from these 9 letters? There is no letter which must be used in every word. You can use only these 9 letters and a letter cannot be used more than once in any word (you may use 3 E's). It's possible to make one 9-letter word.

Score: 20 words or more – EXCELLENT

15 words or more – VERY GOOD

10 words or more – GOOD

Hint: don't forget the plural forms of words, for example dart is 1 word and darts is a 2nd word. It's possible to make 197 words of 4 or more letters. (See following page for answers).

R	E	E
T	E	D
A	S	P

Your Answers:

1. adept	51. pars	101. rates	151. stead
2. adepts	52. parse	102. rats	152. steed
3. aped	53. parsed	103. read	153. steep
4. apes	54. part	104. reads	154. steeped
5. apse	55. parted	105. reap	155. steeper
6. Ares	56. parts	106. reaped	156. steer
7. arts	57. past	107. reaps	157. steered
8. aster	58. paste	108. reds	158. step
9. dare	59. pasted	109. reed	159. stere
10. dares	60. pate	110. reeds	160. strap
11. dart	61. pated	111. repast	161. tads
12. darts	62. pates	112. repeat	162. tape
13. date	63. pats	113. repeated	163. taped
14. dater	64. pear	114. repeats	164. taper
15. dates	65. pears	115. reps	165. tapered
16. dear	66. peas	116. rest	166. tapers
17. dearest	67. peat	117. rested	167. tapes
18. dears	68. pederast	118. sate	168. taps
19. deep	69. peer	119. sated	169. tare
20. deeper	70. peered	120. sear	170. tared
21. deepest	71. peers	121. seared	171. tares
22. deeps	72. pert	122. seat	172. tarp
23. deer	73. peseta	123. seated	173. tarps
24. depart	74. pest	124. sedate	174. tars
25. departs	75. pester	125. seed	175. tear
26. desert	76. pestered	126. seep	176. teared
27. <u>desperate</u>	77. petard	127. seeped	177. tears
28. deter	78. petards	128. seer	178. teas
29. deters	79. peter	129. septa	179. tease
30. drape	80. petered	130. sera	180. teased
31. drapes	81. peters	131. serape	181. teaser
32. eared	82. pets	132. sere	182. teed
33. ears	83. prate	133. spade	183. tees
34. ease	84. prated	134. spader	184. tepee
35. eased	85. prates	135. spar	185. tepees
36. east	86. predate	136. spare	186. terse
37. Easter	87. predates	137. spared	187. trade
38. eater	88. preset	138. spat	188. trades
39. eats	89. rads	139. spate	189. trap
40. epee	90. rape	140. spear	190. traps
41. epees	91. raped	141. speared	191. tread
42. erase	92. rapes	142. sped	192. treads
43. erased	93. raps	143. speed	193. tree
44. Erse	94. rapt	144. speeder	194. treed
45. ester	95. rase	145. sprat	195. trees
46. padre	96. rased	146. spread	196. tsade
47. pads	97. rasp	147. spree	197. tsar
48. pare	98. rasped	148. star	
49. pared	99. rate	149. stare	
50. pares	100. rated	150. stared	

72

#37

How many words can you make from these 9 letters? There is no letter which must be used in every word. You can use only these 9 letters and a letter cannot be used more than once in any word (you may use 3 D's). It's possible to make one 9-letter word.

Score: 20 words or more – EXCELLENT

   15 words or more – VERY GOOD

   10 words or more – GOOD

Hint: don't forget the plural forms of words, for example ace is 1 word and aces is a 2nd word. It's possible to make 148 words of 3 or more letters. (See following page for answers).

A	R	D
E	I	D
C	S	D

Your Answers: _____ _____ _____

_____ _____ _____ _____

_____ _____ _____ _____

_____ _____ _____ _____

_____ _____ _____ _____

_____ _____ _____ _____

_____ _____ _____ _____

_____ _____ _____ _____

_____ _____ _____ _____

_____ _____ _____ _____

_____ _____ _____ _____

1. ace	38. cads	75. dicer	112. rase
2. aced	39. car	76. dicers	113. rased
3. aces	40. card	77. dices	114. read
4. acid	41. carded	78. did	115. reads
5. acids	42. cards	79. die	116. red
6. acre	43. care	80. died	117. reds
7. acres	44. cared	81. dies	118. reis
8. acrid	45. cares	82. dire	119. rice
9. add	46. caries	83. disc	120. riced
10. added	47. cars	84. discard	121. rices
11. adder	48. case	85. discarded	122. rid
12. adders	49. cased	86. disced	123. ridded
13. adds	50. cedar	87. dread	124. ride
14. ads	51. cedars	88. dreads	125. rides
15. aid	52. cedi	89. dried	126. rids
16. aide	53. cedis	90. dries	127. rise
17. aided	54. cider	91. ear	128. sac
18. aider	55. ciders	92. ears	129. sacred
19. aides	56. cir	93. era	130. sad
20. aids	57. cried	94. ice	131. sadder
21. air	58. cries	95. iced	132. said
22. aired	59. dace	96. ices	133. sari
23. airs	60. daces	97. idea	134. scad
24. arc	61. dad	98. ideas	135. scar
25. arced	62. daddies	99. ides	136. scare
26. arcs	63. dads	100. ids	137. scared
27. are	64. Dai	101. ire	138. sea
28. Ares	65. Dais	102. race	139. sear
29. arid	66. dais	103. raced	140. sec
30. Aries	67. dare	104. races	141. sera
31. arise	68. dared	105. rad	142. sic
32. aside	69. dares	106. rads	143. side
33. cad	70. dead	107. raid	144. sidecar
34. caddie	71. dear	108. raided	145. sided
35. caddied	72. dears	109. raids	146. sir
36. caddies	73. dice	110. raise	147. sire
37. cadre	74. diced	111. raised	148. sired

#38

How many words can you make from these 9 letters? There is no letter which must be used in every word. You can use only these 9 letters and a letter cannot be used more than once in any word (you may use 2 D's). It's possible to make one 9-letter word.

Score: 20 words or more – EXCELLENT
    15 words or more – VERY GOOD
    10 words or more – GOOD

It's possible to make 191 words of 3 or more letters. (See following page for answers).

N	A	W
E	D	R
G	D	O

Your Answers:

1. add	49. dower	97. groaned	145. roan
2. adder	50. down	98. grow	146. rod
3. ado	51. downed	99. grown	147. rode
4. adore	52. downer	100. nae	148. roe
5. adored	53. downgrade	101. nag	149. row
6. adorn	54. drag	102. nard	150. rowan
7. adorned	55. dragon	103. near	151. rowed
8. aeon	56. draw	104. Negro	152. wad
9. age	57. drawn	105. nerd	153. wade
10. aged	58. dread	106. New	154. waded
11. ager	59. drew	107. new	155. wader
12. ago	60. drone	108. nod	156. wag
13. and	61. droned	109. nodder	157. wage
14. anew	62. drown	110. node	158. waged
15. anger	63. drowned	111. nor	159. wager
16. anode	64. ear	112. now	160. wagon
17. are	65. earn	113. oar	161. wagoned
18. argon	66. ego	114. oared	162. wan
19. awe	67. end	115. odd	163. wand
20. awed	68. endow	116. odder	164. wander
21. awn	69. eon	117. ode	165. wane
22. awned	70. era	118. ogre	166. waned
23. dad	71. erg	119. one	167. war
24. dado	72. ergo	120. onward	168. ward
25. dag	73. gad	121. orange	169. warded
26. dander	74. gander	122. ore	170. warden
27. Dane	75. gar	123. oread	171. ware
28. danger	76. garden	124. organ	172. wared
29. dare	77. gear	125. owe	173. warn
30. dared	78. gnaw	126. owed	174. warned
31. darn	79. gnawed	127. own	175. wean
32. darned	80. gnawer	128. owned	176. wear
33. dawn	81. goad	129. owner	177. wed
34. dawned	82. goaded	130. rad	178. wen
35. dead	83. god	131. radon	179. wend
36. dean	84. gonad	132. rag	180. woad
37. dear	85. gone	133. rage	181. woe
38. den	86. goner	134. raged	182. won
39. dew	87. gore	135. ran	183. wonder
40. dodge	88. gored	136. rand	184. word
41. doe	89. gown	137. rang	185. wordage
42. doer	90. gowned	138. range	186. worded
43. dog	91. grad	139. ranged	187. wore
44. doge	92. grade	140. raw	188. worn
45. don	93. graded	141. read	189. wren
46. done	94. grand	142. red	190. wrong
47. dong	95. grew	143. rend	191. wronged
48. dowager	96. groan	144. road	

#39

How many words can you make from these 9 letters? There is no letter which must be used in every word. You can use only these 9 letters and a letter cannot be used more than once in any word (you may use 2 A's). It's possible to make one 9-letter word.

Score: 20 words or more – EXCELLENT

15 words or more – VERY GOOD

10 words or more – GOOD

Hint: don't forget the plural forms of words, for example act is 1 word and acts is a 2nd word. It's possible to make 144 words of 3 or more letters. (See following page for answers).

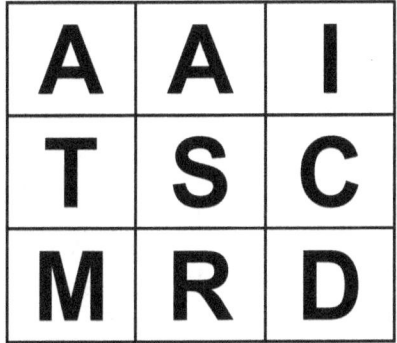

Your Answers:

_____   _____   _____
_____   _____   _____
_____   _____   _____
_____   _____   _____
_____   _____   _____
_____   _____   _____
_____   _____   _____
_____   _____   _____
_____   _____   _____
_____   _____   _____

1. acid	37. card	73. maids	109. sat
2. acids	38. cards	74. mar	110. scad
3. acrid	39. cars	75. mars	111. scam
4. act	40. cart	76. mart	112. scar
5. acts	41. carts	77. marts	113. scat
6. admit	42. cast	78. mast	114. scram
7. admits	43. cat	79. mastic	115. sic
8. ads	44. cats	80. mat	116. sir
9. aid	45. cir	81. mats	117. sit
10. aids	46. cram	82. mica	118. sitar
11. aim	47. crams	83. micas	119. smart
12. aims	48. Dai	84. micra	120. stadia
13. air	49. Dais	85. mid	121. staid
14. airs	50. dam	86. Midas	122. stair
15. amid	51. dams	87. midst	123. star
16. amidst	52. dart	88. mist	124. stir
17. amir	53. darts	89. racism	125. stria
18. amirs	54. data	90. racist	126. tad
19. arc	55. dicta	91. rad	127. tads
20. arcs	56. dim	92. rads	128. Tai
21. aria	57. dims	93. raid	129. Tais
22. arias	58. dirt	94. raids	130. tar
23. arid	59. disarm	95. ram	131. tarmac
24. arm	60. disc	96. Rama	132. tarmacs
25. arms	61. dram	97. rams	133. tars
26. art	62. drama	98. rat	134. tarsi
27. arts	63. dramatics	99. rats	135. tiara
28. astir	64. drams	100. rid	136. tic
29. atria	65. drastic	101. rids	137. tics
30. cad	66. ids	102. rim	138. tis
31. cads	67. ism	103. rims	139. tram
32. cam	68. its	104. sac	140. trams
33. cams	69. mad	105. sacra	141. triad
34. car	70. madras	106. sad	142. trim
35. carat	71. mads	107. said	143. trims
36. carats	72. maid	108. sari	144. tsar

#40

How many words can you make from these 9 letters? There is no letter which must be used in every word. You can use only these 9 letters and a letter cannot be used more than once in any word (you may use 2 E's). It's possible to make one 9-letter word.

Score: 20 words or more – EXCELLENT

     15 words or more – VERY GOOD

     10 words or more – GOOD

Hint: don't forget the plural forms of words, for example horn is 1 word and horns is a 2nd word. It's possible to make 183 words of 4 or more letters. (See following page for answers).

A	N	R
O	E	S
H	E	P

Your Answers:

1. aeon	47. hone	93. peens	139. roans
2. aeons	48. hones	94. peer	140. roes
3. aper	49. hope	95. peers	141. rope
4. apes	50. hoper	96. penes	142. ropes
5. apron	51. hopes	97. pens	143. rose
6. aprons	52. hops	98. peon	144. sane
7. apse	53. horn	99. person	145. saner
8. Ares	54. horns	100. persona	146. sear
9. arose	55. horse	101. personae	147. seen
10. arson	56. hose	102. peso	148. seep
11. ashen	57. Hosea	103. phase	149. seer
12. ashore	58. nape	104. phone	150. sera
13. aspen	59. naps	105. phones	151. serape
14. earn	60. nares	106. phrase	152. seraph
15. earns	61. near	107. pone	153. sere
16. earphone	62. nears	108. pones	154. shape
17. earphones	63. noes	109. pons	155. shaper
18. ears	64. nope	110. pore	156. share
19. ease	65. Norse	111. pores	157. sharp
20. erase	66. nose	112. porn	158. sharpen
21. eros	67. nosh	113. pose	159. shear
22. Erse	68. nosher	114. poser	160. sheen
23. Hans	69. oars	115. posh	161. sheep
24. haps	70. ones	116. preen	162. sheer
25. hare	71. open	117. preens	163. Sherpa
26. hares	72. opens	118. prone	164. shoe
27. harp	73. opera	119. pros	165. shone
28. harps	74. orphan	120. prose	166. shop
29. hasp	75. orphans	121. ranee	167. shore
30. heap	76. pane	122. ranees	168. shorn
31. heaps	77. panes	123. rape	169. snap
32. hear	78. pans	124. rapes	170. snare
33. hears	79. pare	125. raps	171. sneer
34. hearse	80. pares	126. rase	172. snore
35. hens	81. pars	127. rash	173. soap
36. here	82. parse	128. rasp	174. soar
37. hereon	83. parson	129. reap	175. sonar
38. hero	84. paseo	130. reaps	176. sore
39. heroes	85. peahen	131. reason	177. span
40. heron	86. peahens	132. repose	178. spar
41. herons	87. pean	133. reps	179. spare
42. herpes	88. peans	134. resh	180. spear
43. hers	89. pear	135. rhea	181. sphere
44. hoarse	90. pears	136. rheas	182. spore
45. hoer	91. peas	137. rhos	183. spree
46. hoes	92. peen	138. roan	

#41

How many words can you make from these 9 letters? There is no letter which must be used in every word. You can use only these 9 letters and a letter cannot be used more than once in any word (you may use 2 I's). It's possible to make one 9-letter word.

Score: 20 words or more – EXCELLENT
  15 words or more – VERY GOOD
  10 words or more – GOOD

It's possible to make 197 words of 3 or more letters. (See following page for answers).

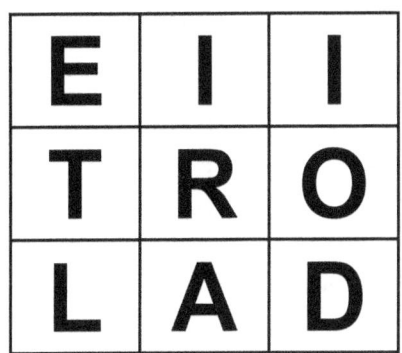

Your Answers: _____ _____ _____

_____ _____ _____ _____

_____ _____ _____ _____

_____ _____ _____ _____

_____ _____ _____ _____

_____ _____ _____ _____

_____ _____ _____ _____

_____ _____ _____ _____

_____ _____ _____ _____

_____ _____ _____ _____

_____ _____ _____ _____

_____ _____ _____ _____

_____ _____ _____ _____

1. ado	51. dote	101. oar	151. Tai
2. adore	52. doter	102. oared	152. tail
3. adroit	53. ear	103. oat	153. tailed
4. aid	54. earl	104. ode	154. tailor
5. aide	55. eat	105. oil	155. tailored
6. aider	56. edit	106. oiled	156. tale
7. ail	57. editorial	107. oiler	157. tali
8. ailed	58. era	108. oilier	158. tar
9. air	59. eta	109. old	159. tare
10. aired	60. idea	110. older	160. tared
11. alder	61. ideal	111. oldie	161. taro
12. ale	62. idiot	112. oral	162. tea
13. alert	63. idle	113. orate	163. teal
14. alit	64. idler	114. orated	164. tear
15. aloe	65. idol	115. ordeal	165. tidal
16. alter	66. ilea	116. ore	166. tide
17. alto	67. iota	117. oriel	167. tidier
18. are	68. irate	118. rad	168. tie
19. arid	69. ire	119. radii	169. tied
20. aril	70. lad	120. radio	170. tier
21. ariled	71. lade	121. raid	171. tilde
22. art	72. laid	122. rail	172. tile
23. ate	73. lair	123. railed	173. tiled
24. Dai	74. lard	124. rat	174. tiler
25. dal	75. late	125. rate	175. tirade
26. dale	76. later	126. rated	176. tire
27. dare	77. lea	127. ratio	177. tired
28. dart	78. lead	128. read	178. toad
29. date	79. led	129. real	179. toe
30. dater	80. lei	130. red	180. toea
31. deal	81. Leo	131. retail	181. toed
32. dealt	82. leotard	132. rial	182. toil
33. dear	83. let	133. rid	183. toiled
34. deli	84. liar	134. ride	184. toiler
35. deliria	85. lid	135. riel	185. told
36. delta	86. lie	136. rile	186. tor
37. derail	87. lied	137. riled	187. tore
38. detail	88. lira	138. riot	188. tori
39. dial	89. lire	139. rioted	189. trade
40. dialer	90. lit	140. rite	190. trail
41. die	91. liter	141. road	191. trailed
42. diet	92. litre	142. rod	192. tread
43. dilate	93. load	143. rode	193. triad
44. dire	94. loader	144. roe	194. trial
45. dirt	95. lode	145. roil	195. tried
46. doe	96. loiter	146. roiled	196. trio
47. doer	97. lord	147. role	197. trod
48. dole	98. lore	148. rot	
49. dolt	99. lot	149. rote	
50. dot	100. loti	150. tad	

#42

How many words can you make from these 9 letters? There is no letter which must be used in every word. You can use only these 9 letters and a letter cannot be used more than once in any word (you may use 2 O's). It's possible to make one 9-letter word.

Score: 20 words or more – EXCELLENT

    15 words or more – VERY GOOD

    10 words or more – GOOD

It's possible to make 173 words of 3 or more letters. (See following page for answers).

Your Answers:

1. aeon	45. late	89. mean	133. noel
2. ail	46. Latin	90. meant	134. not
3. ailment	47. Latino	91. meat	135. note
4. aim	48. lea	92. melon	136. oat
5. ale	49. lean	93. melt	137. oil
6. alien	50. lei	94. men	138. oleo
7. aliment	51. lemon	95. menial	139. olio
8. aline	52. lent	96. mental	140. omen
9. alit	53. lento	97. met	141. omit
10. aloe	54. Leo	98. metal	142. one
11. alone	55. let	99. mien	143. onto
12. alto	56. liane	100. mil	144. oolite
13. amen	57. lie	101. mile	145. Tai
14. amine	58. lien	102. milt	146. tail
15. anole	59. lime	103. min	147. Taino
16. ant	60. limn	104. mina	148. tale
17. ante	61. limo	105. mine	149. tali
18. anti	62. line	106. mint	150. talon
19. ate	63. lint	107. mite	151. tame
20. atom	64. lion	108. moan	152. Tamil
21. atone	65. lit	109. moat	153. tan
22. eat	66. loam	110. moil	154. tea
23. elation	67. loan	111. mol	155. teal
24. elm	68. loin	112. mole	156. team
25. emit	69. lone	113. molt	157. ten
26. emotion	70. loom	114. molten	158. tie
27. emotional	71. loon	115. Monel	159. tile
28. entail	72. loot	116. mono	160. time
29. eolian	73. lot	117. moo	161. tin
30. eon	74. loti	118. moon	162. tine
31. eta	75. lotion	119. moonlit	163. toe
32. ilea	76. mail	120. moot	164. toea
33. inlet	77. main	121. mot	165. toenail
34. inmate	78. male	122. mote	166. toil
35. into	79. maloti	123. motel	167. tom
36. ion	80. malt	124. motile	168. tome
37. iota	81. man	125. motion	169. ton
38. item	82. mane	126. nae	170. tonal
39. lain	83. manito	127. nail	171. tone
40. lam	84. mantel	128. name	172. too
41. lame	85. mantle	129. neat	173. tool
42. lament	86. mat	130. net	
43. lane	87. mate	131. nil	
44. Lao	88. meal	132. nit	

#43

How many words can you make from these 9 letters? There is no letter which must be used in every word. You can use only these 9 letters and a letter cannot be used more than once in any word (you may use 2 E's). It's possible to make one 9-letter word.

Score: 20 words or more – EXCELLENT
     15 words or more – VERY GOOD
     10 words or more – GOOD

Hint: don't forget the plural forms of words, for example earn is 1 word and earns is a 2nd word. It's possible to make 195 words of 4 or more letters. (See following page for answers).

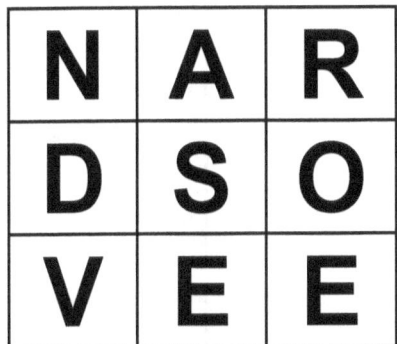

Your Answers: _____ _____ _____

1. adore	50. eased	99. odes	148. savor
2. adores	51. eaves	100. ones	149. savored
3. adorn	52. Eden	101. oread	150. sear
4. adorns	53. endear	102. oven	151. seared
5. adverse	54. endears	103. ovens	152. sedan
6. aeon	55. endeavor	104. over	153. Seder
7. aeons	56. endeavors	105. overed	154. seed
8. anode	57. endorse	106. overs	155. seen
9. anodes	58. ends	107. radon	156. seer
10. Ares	59. erase	108. rads	157. send
11. arose	60. erased	109. rand	158. sender
12. arson	61. erode	110. ranee	159. sene
13. aver	62. erodes	111. ranees	160. sera
14. avers	63. Eros	112. rase	161. sere
15. averse	64. Erse	113. rased	162. serve
16. avos	65. evade	114. rave	163. served
17. Dane	66. evader	115. raved	164. servo
18. Danes	67. evades	116. raven	165. seven
19. dare	68. even	117. ravened	166. sever
20. dares	69. evens	118. ravens	167. snare
21. darn	70. ever	119. raves	168. snared
22. darns	71. eves	120. read	169. sneer
23. dean	72. nard	121. reads	170. snore
24. deans	73. nares	122. reason	171. snored
25. dear	74. nave	123. reasoned	172. soar
26. dears	75. naves	124. reds	173. soared
27. deer	76. near	125. reed	174. soda
28. dens	77. neared	126. reeds	175. sonar
29. dense	78. nears	127. rend	176. sore
30. denser	79. need	128. rends	177. vane
31. doer	80. needs	129. revs	178. vanes
32. doers	81. nerd	130. road	179. vans
33. does	82. nerds	131. roads	180. vase
34. done	83. nerve	132. roan	181. Veda
35. dons	84. nerved	133. roans	182. Vedas
36. dose	85. nerves	134. rode	183. veer
37. doser	86. never	135. rods	184. veers
38. dove	87. node	136. roes	185. vena
39. doves	88. nodes	137. rose	186. venae
40. drone	89. nods	138. rove	187. vend
41. drones	90. noes	139. roved	188. vender
42. drove	91. Norse	140. roves	189. venders
43. droves	92. nose	141. sand	190. vendor
44. eared	93. nosed	142. sander	191. vendors
45. earn	94. nova	143. sane	192. vends
46. earned	95. novae	144. saner	193. verse
47. earns	96. novas	145. save	194. versed
48. ears	97. oared	146. saved	195. verso
49. ease	98. oars	147. saver	

#44

How many words can you make from these 9 letters? There is no letter which must be used in every word. You can use only these 9 letters and a letter cannot be used more than once in any word (you may use 2 E's). It's possible to make one 9-letter word.

Score: 20 words or more – EXCELLENT

     15 words or more – VERY GOOD

     10 words or more – GOOD

It's possible to make 156 words of 4 or more letters. (See following page for answers).

N	B	A
L	D	R
U	E	E

Your Answers:

1. abed	40. blend	79. eared	118. lured
2. able	41. blender	80. earl	119. nard
3. abler	42. blue	81. earn	120. near
4. alder	43. blued	82. earned	121. neared
5. alee	44. bluer	83. Eden	122. nebula
6. bade	45. blunder	84. eland	123. nebulae
7. bald	46. blur	85. elder	124. nebular
8. balder	47. brad	86. elude	125. need
9. bale	48. bran	87. enable	126. nerd
10. baled	49. brand	88. enabled	127. neural
11. baleen	50. bread	89. enabler	128. nude
12. baler	51. bred	90. endear	129. nurd
13. band	52. breed	91. endue	130. rand
14. bane	53. bundle	92. endurable	131. ranee
15. bard	54. bundler	93. endure	132. read
16. bare	55. burden	94. enure	133. real
17. bared	56. burl	95. lade	134. rebel
18. barn	57. burled	96. laden	135. reed
19. baud	58. burn	97. land	136. reel
20. bead	59. burned	98. lane	137. renal
21. beadle	60. dale	99. lard	138. rend
22. bean	61. Dane	100. laree	139. rube
23. beaned	62. dare	101. laud	140. ruble
24. bear	63. darn	102. lauder	141. rude
25. beard	64. daub	103. launder	142. rued
26. beau	65. dauber	104. lead	143. rule
27. been	66. deal	105. leaden	144. ruled
28. beer	67. dealer	106. lean	145. rune
29. bend	68. dean	107. leaned	146. ulna
30. bender	69. dear	108. leaner	147. ulnae
31. blade	70. debar	109. learn	148. ulnar
32. bland	71. deer	110. learned	149. unable
33. blander	72. drab	111. leer	150. unbar
34. blare	73. drub	112. lend	151. under
35. blared	74. dual	113. lender	152. unread
36. blear	75. duel	114. lube	153. unreal
37. bleared	76. dueler	115. lubed	154. urban
38. bled	77. dune	116. lunar	155. urbane
39. bleed	78. durable	117. lure	156. urea

#45

How many words can you make from these 9 letters? Every word must contain the letter "E". You can use only these 9 letters and a letter cannot be used more than once in any word (you may use 2 E's). It's possible to make three 9-letter words.

Score: 20 words or more – EXCELLENT

15 words or more – VERY GOOD

10 words or more – GOOD

Hint: don't forget the plural forms of words, for example cent is 1 word and cents is a 2nd word. It's possible to make 196 words of 4 or more letters. (See following page for answers).

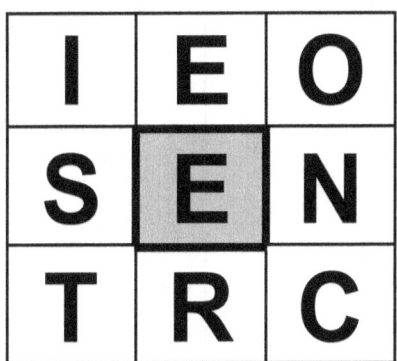

Your Answers:

1. censer	50. eosin	99. recto	148. sneer
2. censor	51. erect	100. rectos	149. snore
3. cent	52. erection	101. rein	150. soiree
4. center	53. <u>erections</u>	102. reins	151. sore
5. centers	54. erects	103. reis	152. sortie
6. centre	55. Erie	104. rent	153. steer
7. centres	56. Eros	105. rents	154. stein
8. cents	57. erotic	106. <u>resection</u>	155. steno
9. Ceres	58. Erse	107. resent	156. stere
10. cerise	59. escort	108. resin	157. stereo
11. cero	60. esoteric	109. rest	158. stern
12. ceros	61. ester	110. rice	159. stone
13. cistern	62. ices	111. rices	160. stoner
14. cite	63. incest	112. rinse	161. stonier
15. cites	64. inert	113. rise	162. store
16. coiner	65. insect	114. risen	163. teen
17. cone	66. insert	115. rite	164. teens
18. cones	67. inset	116. rites	165. tees
19. conies	68. inter	117. roes	166. tenor
20. core	69. inters	118. rose	167. tenors
21. cores	70. nest	119. rote	168. tens
22. cornet	71. nets	120. rotes	169. tense
23. cornets	72. nice	121. scene	170. tenser
24. corniest	73. nicer	122. scent	171. tensor
25. corset	74. nicest	123. scone	172. tern
26. cosier	75. niece	124. score	173. terns
27. cosine	76. nieces	125. scoter	174. terse
28. cote	77. niter	126. scree	175. tier
29. coterie	78. niters	127. screen	176. tiers
30. cotes	79. nitre	128. secret	177. ties
31. Cree	80. noes	129. <u>secretion</u>	178. tine
32. Crees	81. noise	130. sect	179. tines
33. crest	82. Norse	131. section	180. tire
34. cretin	83. nose	132. sector	181. tires
35. cretins	84. nosier	133. seen	182. toes
36. cries	85. note	134. seer	183. tone
37. crone	86. noter	135. seine	184. toner
38. crones	87. notes	136. seiner	185. toners
39. cronies	88. notice	137. sene	186. tones
40. encore	89. notices	138. senior	187. tonier
41. encores	90. once	139. sent	188. tore
42. enter	91. ones	140. sente	189. Tories
43. enteric	92. onset	141. sere	190. tree
44. enters	93. orient	142. since	191. trees
45. entice	94. orients	143. sincere	192. trice
46. enticer	95. osier	144. sine	193. trices
47. entices	96. recent	145. sire	194. tries
48. entire	97. recite	146. siren	195. trine
49. entries	98. recites	147. site	196. trines

#46

How many words can you make from these 9 letters? There is no letter which must be used in every word. You can use only these 9 letters and a letter cannot be used more than once in any word (you may use 2 E's). It's possible to make one 9-letter word.

Score: 20 words or more – EXCELLENT

15 words or more – VERY GOOD

10 words or more – GOOD

It's possible to make 107 words of 3 or more letters. (See following page for answers).

Your Answers:

1. deity	37. ivy	73. ten
2. deli	38. led	74. tend
3. delve	39. lee	75. tide
4. den	40. lei	76. tidy
5. dent	41. lend	77. tie
6. deny	42. lent	78. tied
7. devil	43. let	79. tilde
8. die	44. levied	80. tile
9. diet	45. levity	81. tiled
10. din	46. levy	82. tin
11. dine	47. ley	83. tine
12. dint	48. lid	84. tined
13. dive	49. lie	85. tiny
14. dye	50. lied	86. veil
15. Eden	51. lien	87. veiled
16. edit	52. line	88. vein
17. eel	53. lined	89. veined
18. elide	54. lint	90. veld
19. elite	55. linty	91. veldt
20. end	56. lit	92. vend
21. endive	57. live	93. vent
22. envied	58. lived	94. vented
23. envy	59. liven	95. vet
24. eve	60. livened	96. vide
25. even	61. lye	97. vie
26. evenly	62. nee	98. vied
27. event	63. need	99. vile
28. evident	64. needy	100. vine
29. evidently	65. net	101. vined
30. evil	66. nevi	102. vinyl
31. eye	67. nil	103. yen
32. eyed	68. nit	104. yet
33. eyelid	69. tee	105. yeti
34. idle	70. teed	106. yield
35. idly	71. teen	107. yin
36. inlet	72. teeny	

#47

How many words can you make from these 9 letters? There is no letter which must be used in every word. You can use only these 9 letters and a letter cannot be used more than once in any word (you may use 2 E's). It's possible to make one 9-letter word.

Score: 20 words or more – EXCELLENT

15 words or more – VERY GOOD

10 words or more – GOOD

Hint: don't forget the plural forms of words, for example eel is 1 word and eels is a 2nd word. It's possible to make an even 100 words of 3 or more letters. Eighteen words contain the letter "X". (See following page for answers).

P	S	O
V	X	I
L	E	E

Your Answers:

_____ _____ _____

_____ _____ _____

_____ _____ _____

_____ _____ _____

_____ _____ _____

_____ _____ _____

_____ _____ _____

_____ _____ _____

_____ _____ _____

1. eel	35. lopes	69. sex
2. eels	36. lops	70. sieve
3. elope	37. lose	71. silo
4. elopes	38. love	72. sip
5. else	39. loves	73. six
6. elves	40. lox	74. sleep
7. epoxies	41. oil	75. slip
8. eve	42. oils	76. sloe
9. eves	43. olive	77. slop
10. evil	44. olives	78. slope
11. evils	45. peel	79. soil
12. exes	46. peels	80. sol
13. exile	47. pelves	81. sole
14. exiles	48. pelvis	82. solve
15. expel	49. peso	83. sop
16. expels	50. pie	84. sox
17. <u>explosive</u>	51. pies	85. spiel
18. expose	52. pile	86. spoil
19. isle	53. piles	87. veil
20. lee	54. pilose	88. veils
21. lees	55. pix	89. vex
22. lei	56. pixel	90. vexes
23. leis	57. plies	91. vie
24. Leo	58. plosive	92. vies
25. levies	59. poi	93. vile
26. lie	60. poise	94. viol
27. lies	61. pole	95. viols
28. lip	62. poles	96. vise
29. lips	63. pose	97. voile
30. lisp	64. pox	98. voiles
31. live	65. poxes	99. vole
32. lives	66. psi	100. voles
33. lop	67. see	
34. lope	68. seep	

#48

How many words can you make from these 9 letters? There is no letter which must be used in every word. You can use only these 9 letters and a letter cannot be used more than once in any word (you may use 2 I's). It's possible to make one 9-letter word.

Score: 20 words or more – EXCELLENT

    15 words or more – VERY GOOD

    10 words or more – GOOD

Hint: don't forget the plural forms of words, for example ace is 1 word and aces is a 2nd word. It's possible to make 120 words of 3 or more letters. (See following page for answers).

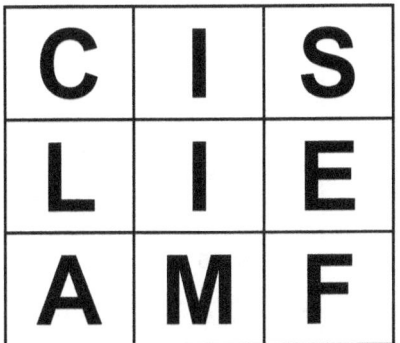

Your Answers:

1. ace	41. false	81. mace
2. aces	42. fame	82. maces
3. acme	43. fames	83. mail
4. ail	44. families	84. mails
5. ails	45. fie	85. male
6. aim	46. file	86. malefic
7. aims	47. files	87. males
8. aisle	48. film	88. malice
9. ale	49. films	89. meal
10. ales	50. fiscal	90. meals
11. alms	51. flame	91. mesa
12. cafe	52. flames	92. mescal
13. cafes	53. flea	93. mica
14. calf	54. fleas	94. micas
15. calm	55. flies	95. mice
16. calms	56. ice	96. mil
17. cam	57. ices	97. mile
18. came	58. ifs	98. miles
19. camel	59. ilea	99. mils
20. camels	60. Islam	100. misfile
21. cams	61. Islamic	101. sac
22. case	62. isle	102. safe
23. cilia	63. lace	103. sail
24. claim	64. laces	104. sale
25. claims	65. lam	105. same
26. clam	66. lame	106. scale
27. clams	67. lames	107. scam
28. clef	68. lams	108. sea
29. clefs	69. lea	109. seal
30. clime	70. leaf	110. seam
31. climes	71. leafs	111. self
32. elf	72. lei	112. semi
33. elm	73. leis	113. sic
34. elms	74. lice	114. silica
35. face	75. lie	115. simile
36. faces	76. lief	116. slam
37. facile	77. lies	117. slice
38. facsimile	78. life	118. slim
39. fail	79. lime	119. slime
40. fails	80. limes	120. smile

#49

How many words can you make from these 9 letters? Every word must contain the letter "A". You can use only these 9 letters and a letter cannot be used more than once in any word. It's possible to make one 9-letter word.

Score: 20 words or more – EXCELLENT
　　　15 words or more – VERY GOOD
　　　10 words or more – GOOD

Hint: don't forget the plural forms of words, for example acre is 1 word and acres is a 2nd word. It's possible to make 161 words of 4 or more letters. (See following page for answers).

Your Answers:

1. aces	42. coast	83. fear	124. satire
2. acre	43. coaster	84. fears	125. scar
3. acres	44. coat	85. feast	126. scare
4. actor	45. coati	86. feat	127. scarf
5. actors	46. coatis	87. feats	128. scat
6. acts	47. coats	88. feta	129. scoria
7. afire	48. coria	89. fiasco	130. scoriae
8. Afro	49. costar	90. fiat	131. scrota
9. Afros	50. craft	91. fiesta	132. sear
10. after	51. crafts	92. fora	133. seat
11. airs	52. crate	93. forecast	134. sera
12. aortic	53. crates	94. iota	135. sitar
13. arcs	54. Croat	95. irate	136. soar
14. Ares	55. Croats	96. oafs	137. sofa
15. Aries	56. ears	97. oars	138. stair
16. arise	57. east	98. oats	139. star
17. arose	58. eats	99. orate	140. stare
18. arts	59. erotica	100. orates	141. stoa
19. ascot	60. face	101. orca	142. stoae
20. aster	61. faces	102. orcas	143. strafe
21. astir	62. facet	103. race	144. stria
22. cafe	63. facets	104. races	145. striae
23. cafes	64. fact	105. raciest	146. taco
24. care	65. factor	106. racist	147. tacos
25. cares	66. factories	107. raft	148. Tais
26. caret	67. factors	108. rafts	149. tare
27. carets	68. facts	109. raise	150. tares
28. caries	69. fair	110. rase	151. taro
29. cars	70. fairest	111. rate	152. taros
30. cart	71. fairs	112. rates	153. tars
31. carts	72. farce	113. ratio	154. tarsi
32. case	73. farces	114. ratios	155. tear
33. cast	74. fare	115. rats	156. tears
34. caste	75. fares	116. react	157. teas
35. caster	76. faro	117. reacts	158. toea
36. castor	77. faros	118. recta	159. trace
37. cater	78. fast	119. roast	160. traces
38. caters	79. faster	120. safe	161. tsar
39. cats	80. fate	121. safer	
40. ciao	81. fates	122. sari	
41. coarse	82. fats	123. sate	

#50

How many words can you make from these 9 letters? Every word must contain the letter "E". You can use only these 9 letters and a letter cannot be used more than once in any word. It's possible to make one 9-letter word.

Score: 20 words or more – EXCELLENT

    15 words or more – VERY GOOD

    10 words or more – GOOD

It's possible to make 167 words of 4 or more letters. (See following page for answers).

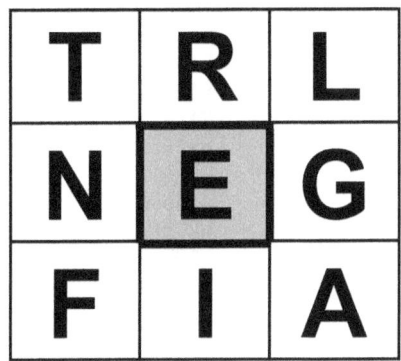

Your Answers:

1. afire	43. feting	85. infer	127. ratline
2. after	44. file	86. inflate	128. real
3. agent	45. filet	87. inflater	129. regain
4. ager	46. filter	88. ingrate	130. regal
5. agile	47. finagle	89. inlet	131. reign
6. aigret	48. finagler	90. integral	132. rein
7. alert	49. finale	91. inter	133. relating
8. alerting	50. fine	92. irate	134. reliant
9. alien	51. finer	93. lager	135. renal
10. aligner	52. finger	94. lane	136. rent
11. aline	53. fire	95. large	137. rental
12. alter	54. flange	96. late	138. retail
13. altering	55. flare	97. later	139. retain
14. angel	56. flea	98. latrine	140. retina
15. anger	57. flier	99. leaf	141. retinal
16. angle	58. fragile	100. leafing	142. riel
17. ante	59. frena	101. lean	143. rife
18. antler	60. fret	102. learn	144. rifle
19. argent	61. frigate	103. learnt	145. rile
20. earing	62. fringe	104. left	146. ringlet
21. earl	63. Gael	105. lent	147. rite
22. earn	64. gainer	106. liane	148. tale
23. eating	65. gaiter	107. lief	149. tangle
24. elating	66. gale	108. lien	150. tare
25. engraft	67. garnet	109. life	151. teal
26. entail	68. gate	110. lifter	152. tear
27. fainter	69. gater	111. linage	153. tearing
28. falter	70. gear	112. line	154. tern
29. faltering	71. gelatin	113. linear	155. tier
30. fare	72. gelt	114. liner	156. tiger
31. fate	73. genial	115. linger	157. tile
32. fear	74. genital	116. lire	158. tiler
33. fearing	75. gent	117. liter	159. tine
34. feat	76. glare	118. litre	160. tinge
35. feign	77. glean	119. nailer	161. tingle
36. feint	78. glen	120. near	162. tingler
37. felt	79. granite	121. neat	163. tire
38. felting	80. grate	122. niter	164. triage
39. feral	81. great	123. nitre	165. triangle
40. fern	82. grief	124. rage	166. trifle
41. feta	83. ilea	125. range	167. trine
42. fetal	84. inert	126. rate	

#51

How many words can you make from these 9 letters? There is no letter which must be used in every word. You can use only these 9 letters and a letter cannot be used more than once in any word. It's possible to make one 9-letter word.

Score: 20 words or more – EXCELLENT

    15 words or more – VERY GOOD

    10 words or more – GOOD

Hint: don't forget the plural forms of words, for example arm is 1 word and arms is a 2nd word. It's possible to make 181 words of 3 or more letters. (See following page for answers).

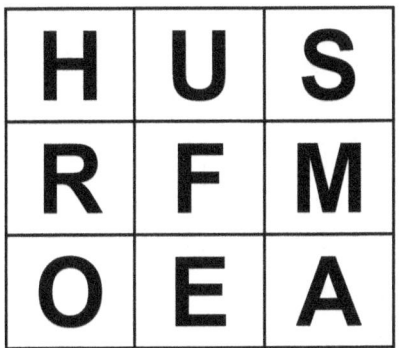

Your Answers:

1. afresh	47. fora	93. hues	139. roes
2. Afro	48. fore	94. hum	140. rose
3. Afros	49. form	95. humor	141. rouse
4. ahem	50. forms	96. humors	142. rue
5. amour	51. forum	97. hums	143. rues
6. amours	52. forums	98. mar	144. rum
7. amuse	53. four	99. mare	145. rums
8. amuser	54. frame	100. mares	146. ruse
9. are	55. frames	101. mars	147. rush
10. Ares	56. fresh	102. marsh	148. safe
11. arm	57. fro	103. maser	149. safer
12. arms	58. from	104. mash	150. same
13. arose	59. fume	105. mesa	151. sea
14. arouse	60. fumes	106. mesh	152. seam
15. arum	61. fur	107. more	153. sear
16. ash	62. furs	108. mores	154. sera
17. ashore	63. fuse	109. moue	155. serf
18. Aum	64. ham	110. moues	156. serum
19. Aums	65. hams	111. mouse	157. sham
20. ear	66. hare	112. muse	158. shame
21. ears	67. harem	113. mush	159. share
22. emu	68. hares	114. musher	160. she
23. emus	69. harm	115. oaf	161. sheaf
24. era	70. harms	116. oafs	162. shear
25. Eros	71. has	117. oar	163. shoe
26. fame	72. hear	118. oars	164. shofar
27. fames	73. hears	119. ohm	165. shore
28. famous	74. hem	120. ohms	166. smear
29. far	75. hems	121. ore	167. soar
30. fare	76. her	122. our	168. sofa
31. fares	77. hero	123. ours	169. some
32. farm	78. hers	124. ram	170. sore
33. farmhouse	79. hoarse	125. rams	171. sour
34. farms	80. hoe	126. rase	172. sue
35. faro	81. hoer	127. rash	173. suer
36. faros	82. hoes	128. ream	174. sum
37. fear	83. home	129. reams	175. sumo
38. fears	84. homer	130. resh	176. sure
39. femora	85. homers	131. rhea	177. surf
40. femur	86. homes	132. rheas	178. urea
41. femurs	87. horse	133. rheum	179. use
42. foam	88. hose	134. rho	180. user
43. foams	89. hour	135. rhos	181. usher
44. foe	90. hours	136. roam	
45. foes	91. house	137. roams	
46. for	92. hue	138. roe	

#52

How many words can you make from these 9 letters? There is no letter which must be used in every word. You can use only these 9 letters and a letter cannot be used more than once in any word (you may use 2 S's). It's possible to make one 9-letter word.

Score: 20 words or more – EXCELLENT

    15 words or more – VERY GOOD

    10 words or more – GOOD

Hint: don't forget the plural forms of words, for example flea is 1 word and fleas is a 2nd word. It's possible to make 180 words of 4 or more letters. (See following page for answers).

S	E	S
L	I	A
V	F	T

Your Answers:

1. ails	46. flea	91. salve	136. tails
2. aisle	47. fleas	92. salves	137. Tais
3. aisles	48. flies	93. sate	138. tale
4. ales	49. flit	94. sates	139. tales
5. alit	50. flits	95. save	140. tali
6. alive	51. ilea	96. saves	141. tassel
7. asset	52. isle	97. seal	142. teal
8. east	53. isles	98. seals	143. teals
9. eats	54. islet	99. seas	144. teas
10. evil	55. islets	100. seat	145. ties
11. evils	56. itself	101. seats	146. tile
12. fail	57. lass	102. self	147. tiles
13. fails	58. lassie	103. sets	148. vale
14. false	59. last	104. siesta	149. vales
15. falsest	60. lasts	105. sift	150. valet
16. fast	61. late	106. sifts	151. valets
17. fasts	62. lave	107. silt	152. valise
18. fate	63. laves	108. silts	153. valises
19. fates	64. leaf	109. sisal	154. vase
20. fats	65. leafs	110. site	155. vast
21. feast	66. least	111. sites	156. vats
22. feasts	67. left	112. sits	157. veal
23. feat	68. lefts	113. slat	158. veil
24. feats	69. leis	114. slate	159. veils
25. felt	70. less	115. slates	160. vela
26. felts	71. lest	116. slats	161. vest
27. festal	72. lets	117. Slav	162. vestal
28. festival	73. lief	118. slave	163. vestals
29. festivals	74. lies	119. slaves	164. vests
30. feta	75. life	120. Slavs	165. vets
31. fetal	76. lift	121. sliest	166. vial
32. fiat	77. lifts	122. slit	167. vials
33. fiesta	78. list	123. slits	168. vies
34. fiestas	79. lists	124. stale	169. vile
35. file	80. live	125. stales	170. vilest
36. files	81. lives	126. stave	171. visa
37. filet	82. safe	127. staves	172. visas
38. fils	83. safes	128. steal	173. vise
39. fist	84. safest	129. steals	174. vises
40. fists	85. sail	130. sties	175. vista
41. fits	86. sails	131. stifle	176. vistas
42. five	87. sale	132. stifles	177. vita
43. fives	88. sales	133. stile	178. vitae
44. flat	89. salt	134. stiles	179. vital
45. flats	90. salts	135. tail	180. vitals

#53

How many words can you make from these 9 letters? There is no letter which must be used in every word. You can use only these 9 letters and a letter cannot be used more than once in any word. It's possible to make one 9-letter word.

Score: 20 words or more – EXCELLENT

15 words or more – VERY GOOD

10 words or more – GOOD

Hint: don't forget the plural forms of words, for example fire is 1 word and fires is a 2nd word. It's possible to make 174 words of 4 or more letters. (See following page for answers).

S	N	I
A	E	M
H	R	F

Your Answers:

1. afire	45. fire	89. marine	133. remains
2. afresh	46. fireman	90. marines	134. resh
3. ahem	47. fires	91. mars	135. resin
4. aims	48. firm	92. marsh	136. rhea
5. airmen	49. firms	93. maser	137. rheas
6. airs	50. firs	94. mash	138. rife
7. amen	51. fish	95. mean	139. rime
8. amine	52. fisherman	96. means	140. rimes
9. Amish	53. frame	97. menhir	141. rims
10. anise	54. frames	98. menhirs	142. rinse
11. Ares	55. frena	99. mesa	143. rise
12. Aries	56. fresh	100. mesh	144. risen
13. arise	57. freshman	101. mien	145. safe
14. arisen	58. fries	102. miens	146. safer
15. armies	59. hair	103. mina	147. same
16. arms	60. hairs	104. minas	148. sane
17. ashen	61. hams	105. mine	149. saner
18. ashier	62. hare	106. mines	150. sari
19. earn	63. harem	107. mire	151. seam
20. earns	64. hares	108. mires	152. sear
21. ears	65. harm	109. miser	153. semi
22. emir	66. harms	110. mishear	154. seminar
23. fain	67. hear	111. name	155. sera
24. fair	68. hears	112. namer	156. serf
25. fairs	69. heir	113. names	157. serif
26. fame	70. heirs	114. nares	158. sham
27. fames	71. hems	115. naris	159. shame
28. famine	72. hens	116. near	160. share
29. famines	73. hernia	117. nears	161. sheaf
30. famish	74. hernias	118. rain	162. shear
31. fans	75. hers	119. rains	163. shier
32. fare	76. hire	120. raise	164. shim
33. fares	77. hires	121. ramie	165. shin
34. farm	78. infer	122. rams	166. shine
35. farms	79. infers	123. rani	167. shiner
36. fear	80. inseam	124. ranis	168. shire
37. fears	81. main	125. rase	169. shrine
38. fens	82. mains	126. rash	170. sine
39. fern	83. mane	127. ream	171. sire
40. ferns	84. manes	128. reams	172. siren
41. fine	85. mans	129. rein	173. smear
42. finer	86. manse	130. reins	174. snare
43. fines	87. mare	131. reis	
44. fins	88. mares	132. remain	

#54

How many words can you make from these 9 letters? Every word must contain the letter "A". You can use only these 9 letters and a letter cannot be used more than once in any word. It's possible to make one 9-letter word.

Score: 20 words or more – EXCELLENT
    15 words or more – VERY GOOD
    10 words or more – GOOD

Hint: don't forget the plural forms of words, for example fate is 1 word and fates is a 2nd word. It's possible to make 152 words of 4 or more letters. (See following page for answers).

Your Answers:

1. aeon	39. fasten	77. gloat	115. sate
2. aeons	40. fate	78. gloats	116. seal
3. agent	41. fates	79. gnat	117. seat
4. agents	42. fats	80. gnats	118. slag
5. ages	43. feast	81. goal	119. slang
6. ales	44. feat	82. goals	120. slant
7. aloe	45. feats	83. goat	121. slat
8. aloes	46. festal	84. goats	122. slate
9. aloft	47. feta	85. lags	123. slogan
10. alone	48. fetal	86. lane	124. snag
11. along	49. flag	87. lanes	125. sofa
12. also	50. flagon	88. Laos	126. stag
13. alto	51. flagons	89. last	127. stage
14. altos	52. flags	90. late	128. stale
15. angel	53. flagstone	91. leaf	129. steal
16. angels	54. flan	92. leafs	130. stoa
17. angle	55. flange	93. lean	131. stoae
18. angles	56. flanges	94. leans	132. tags
19. Anglo	57. flat	95. least	133. tale
20. Anglos	58. flats	96. legato	134. tales
21. angst	59. flea	97. legatos	135. talon
22. anole	60. fleas	98. loaf	136. talons
23. anoles	61. float	99. loafs	137. tang
24. ante	62. floats	100. loan	138. tangelo
25. antes	63. foal	101. loans	139. tangelos
26. ants	64. foals	102. nags	140. tangle
27. atone	65. foetal	103. neat	141. tangles
28. atones	66. fontal	104. oafs	142. tango
29. east	67. Gael	105. oats	143. tangos
30. eats	68. Gaels	106. Osage	144. tangs
31. fagot	69. gale	107. safe	145. tans
32. fagots	70. gales	108. sage	146. teal
33. fags	71. gals	109. sago	147. teals
34. false	72. gate	110. sale	148. teas
35. fang	73. gates	111. salon	149. toea
36. fangs	74. glans	112. salt	150. toga
37. fans	75. glean	113. sane	151. togas
38. fast	76. gleans	114. sang	152. tonal

#55

How many words can you make from these 9 letters? There is no letter which must be used in every word. You can use only these 9 letters and a letter cannot be used more than once in any word. It's possible to make one 9-letter word.

Score: 20 words or more – EXCELLENT

    15 words or more – VERY GOOD

    10 words or more – GOOD

Hint: don't forget the plural forms of words, for example fire is 1 word and fires is a 2nd word. It's possible to make 179 words of 4 or more letters. (See following page for answers).

S	H	O
R	G	T
E	I	F

Your Answers:

1. efts	46. frets	91. hoist	136. shrift
2. egis	47. fries	92. hoister	137. sift
3. egos	48. fright	93. horse	138. sifter
4. eight	49. frights	94. hose	139. sigh
5. ergo	50. frog	95. host	140. sigher
6. ergot	51. frost	96. hots	141. sight
7. ergs	52. froth	97. ogre	142. sire
8. Eros	53. froths	98. ogres	143. site
9. ethos	54. gets	99. orgies	144. soft
10. fetish	55. ghost	100. osier	145. softer
11. fight	56. gift	101. other	146. softie
12. fighter	57. gifts	102. others	147. sore
13. fighters	58. girt	103. reis	148. sort
14. fights	59. girth	104. resh	149. sortie
15. figs	60. girths	105. rest	150. stir
16. fire	61. gist	106. rhos	151. store
17. fires	62. goes	107. rife	152. strife
18. firs	63. goiter	108. rifest	153. their
19. first	64. goiters	109. rift	154. theirs
20. firth	65. gore	110. rifts	155. thief
21. firths	66. gores	111. right	156. this
22. fish	67. goriest	112. rights	157. Thor
23. fist	68. gorse	113. rigs	158. those
24. fits	69. gosh	114. riot	159. throe
25. foes	70. Goth	115. riots	160. throes
26. fogies	71. Goths	116. rise	161. tier
27. fogs	72. grief	117. rite	162. tiers
28. foist	73. grist	118. rites	163. ties
29. fore	74. grit	119. roes	164. tiger
30. foresight	75. grits	120. rose	165. tigers
31. forest	76. heft	121. rote	166. tire
32. forge	77. hefts	122. rotes	167. tires
33. forges	78. heir	123. rots	168. toes
34. forget	79. heirs	124. serf	169. togs
35. forgets	80. heist	125. serif	170. tore
36. fort	81. hero	126. shier	171. tori
37. forte	82. hers	127. shift	172. Tories
38. fortes	83. hire	128. shifter	173. tors
39. forth	84. hires	129. shire	174. torsi
40. forties	85. hits	130. shirt	175. tries
41. foster	86. hoer	131. shoe	176. trig
42. freight	87. hoes	132. shore	177. trigs
43. freights	88. hogs	133. short	178. trio
44. fresh	89. hogtie	134. shot	179. trios
45. fret	90. hogties	135. shote	

#56

How many words can you make from these 9 letters? There is no letter which must be used in every word. You can use only these 9 letters and a letter cannot be used more than once in any word (you may use 2 L's and 2 E's). It's possible to make two 9-letter words.

Score: 20 words or more – EXCELLENT

    15 words or more – VERY GOOD

    10 words or more – GOOD

Hint: don't forget the plural forms of words, for example age is 1 word and ages is a 2nd word. It's possible to make 178 words of 3 or more letters. (See following page for answers).

E	A	L
E	R	L
S	G	I

Your Answers: _____ _____ _____

1. aegis	46. era	91. Israel	136. regal
2. aerie	47. erase	92. lag	137. regale
3. aeries	48. ere	93. lager	138. regales
4. age	49. erg	94. lagers	139. reis
5. ager	50. ergs	95. lags	140. relies
6. ages	51. Erie	96. lair	141. rial
7. agile	52. Gael	97. lairs	142. rials
8. agree	53. Gaels	98. laree	143. riel
9. agrees	54. gal	99. larees	144. riels
10. ail	55. gale	100. large	145. rig
11. ails	56. gales	101. laser	146. rigs
12. air	57. gall	102. lea	147. rile
13. airs	58. galleries	103. lease	148. riles
14. aisle	59. galls	104. leaser	149. rill
15. ale	60. gals	105. lee	150. rille
16. alee	61. gar	106. leer	151. rilles
17. ales	62. gars	107. leers	152. rills
18. all	63. gas	108. lees	153. rise
19. allege	64. gear	109. leg	154. sag
20. alleger	65. gears	110. legal	155. sage
21. alleges	66. gee	111. legals	156. sager
22. allergies	67. gel	112. legs	157. sail
23. allies	68. gels	113. lei	158. sale
24. are	69. gill	114. leis	159. sari
25. Ares	70. gills	115. liar	160. sea
26. Aries	71. girl	116. liars	161. seal
27. aril	72. girls	117. lie	162. sealer
28. arils	73. glare	118. liege	163. sear
29. arise	74. glares	119. lieges	164. see
30. eager	75. glee	120. lies	165. seer
31. eagle	76. glees	121. lira	166. sell
32. eagles	77. grail	122. lire	167. seller
33. ear	78. grails	123. lisle	168. sera
34. earl	79. grease	124. rag	169. sere
35. earls	80. grill	125. rage	170. serge
36. ears	81. grille	126. rages	171. serial
37. ease	82. grilles	127. rags	172. siege
38. easel	83. grills	128. rail	173. silage
39. easier	84. grilse	129. rails	174. sill
40. eel	85. ilea	130. raise	175. sir
41. eels	86. ileal	131. rallies	176. sire
42. egis	87. ill	132. rase	177. slag
43. ell	88. ills	133. real	178. slier
44. ells	89. ire	134. reel	
45. else	90. isle	135. reels	

#57

How many words can you make from these 9 letters? There is no letter which must be used in every word. You can use only these 9 letters and a letter cannot be used more than once in any word. It's possible to make one 9-letter word.

Score: 20 words or more – EXCELLENT

    15 words or more – VERY GOOD

    10 words or more – GOOD

It's possible to make 183 words of 4 or more letters. (See following page for answers).

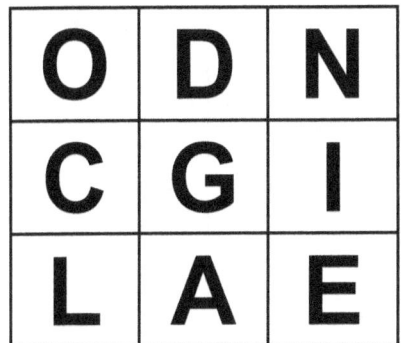

O	D	N
C	G	I
L	A	E

Your Answers:

1. aced	47. coal	93. eland	139. lanced
2. acid	48. coaled	94. eolian	140. land
3. acing	49. coaling	95. Gael	141. lane
4. acne	50. coda	96. Gaelic	142. lead
5. acned	51. code	97. gain	143. leading
6. aeon	52. coding	98. gained	144. lean
7. aged	53. coed	99. gale	145. legion
8. agile	54. coil	100. geld	146. lend
9. aide	55. coiled	101. gelid	147. liane
10. ailed	56. coin	102. genial	148. lice
11. alien	57. coinage	103. genocidal	149. lied
12. align	58. coined	104. gild	150. lien
13. aligned	59. cola	105. glad	151. linage
14. aline	60. cold	106. glade	152. line
15. alined	61. cone	107. glance	153. lined
16. aloe	62. coned	108. glanced	154. lingo
17. alone	63. congeal	109. gland	155. lion
18. along	64. dace	110. glean	156. load
19. angel	65. dale	111. glen	157. loading
20. angelic	66. dance	112. glide	158. loan
21. angle	67. Dane	113. goad	159. loaned
22. angled	68. dangle	114. goal	160. loci
23. Anglo	69. danio	115. goalie	161. lode
24. anode	70. deacon	116. gold	162. lodge
25. anole	71. deal	117. golden	163. loge
26. cadge	72. dealing	118. gonad	164. logic
27. cage	73. dean	119. gonadic	165. loin
28. caged	74. decagon	120. gone	166. lone
29. candle	75. decal	121. iced	167. long
30. cane	76. deign	122. icon	168. longed
31. caned	77. deli	123. idea	169. nail
32. canoe	78. denial	124. ideal	170. nailed
33. canoed	79. dial	125. idle	171. nice
34. cedi	80. dialog	126. idol	172. node
35. ceding	81. dice	127. ilea	173. noel
36. ciao	82. dine	128. Inca	174. ocean
37. clad	83. ding	129. lace	175. Odin
38. clan	84. dingo	130. laced	176. ogle
39. clang	85. docile	131. lacing	177. ogled
40. clanged	86. doge	132. lade	178. oilcan
41. clean	87. dogie	133. laden	179. oiled
42. cling	88. doing	134. lading	180. olden
43. clod	89. dole	135. ladino	181. oldie
44. clog	90. doling	136. laid	182. once
45. clone	91. done	137. lain	183. Oneida
46. cloned	92. dong	138. lance	

#58

How many words can you make from these 9 letters? There is no letter which must be used in every word. You can use only these 9 letters and a letter cannot be used more than once in any word (you may use 2 E's). It's possible to make one 9-letter word.

Score: 20 words or more – EXCELLENT

   15 words or more – VERY GOOD

   10 words or more – GOOD

It's possible to make 197 words of 4 or more letters. (See following page for answers).

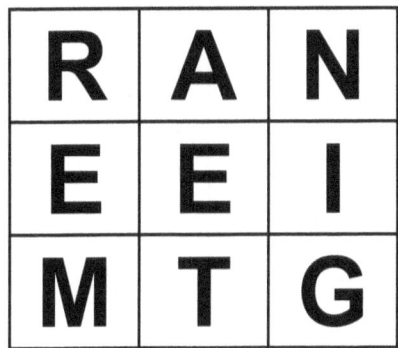

R	A	N
E	E	I
M	T	G

Your Answers:

1. aerie	51. gent	101. meet	151. regimen
2. agent	52. germ	102. meeting	152. regiment
3. ager	53. German	103. mere	153. reign
4. agree	54. germane	104. merge	154. rein
5. airmen	55. germinate	105. merit	155. remain
6. amen	56. giant	106. mete	156. remit
7. amine	57. girt	107. meter	157. rent
8. anger	58. gnat	108. metering	158. retain
9. ante	59. grain	109. meting	159. retina
10. anti	60. gram	110. metre	160. retinae
11. argent	61. granite	111. mien	161. rime
12. arming	62. grant	112. migrant	162. ring
13. eager	63. grate	113. migrate	163. rite
14. earing	64. great	114. mina	164. tame
15. earn	65. green	115. minaret	165. tamer
16. eaten	66. greet	116. mine	166. taming
17. eater	67. grim	117. mint	167. tang
18. eating	68. grime	118. minter	168. tare
19. egret	69. grin	119. mirage	169. taring
20. emigrate	70. grit	120. mire	170. tarn
21. emir	71. image	121. mite	171. team
22. emirate	72. inert	122. miter	172. teaming
23. emit	73. ingrate	123. mitre	173. tear
24. enema	74. inmate	124. name	174. tearing
25. enigma	75. integer	125. namer	175. teeing
26. enrage	76. inter	126. near	176. teem
27. enter	77. irate	127. neat	177. teeming
28. entire	78. item	128. neater	178. teen
29. Erie	79. magi	129. negate	179. term
30. ermine	80. magnet	130. negater	180. terming
31. gain	81. main	131. niter	181. tern
32. gainer	82. mane	132. nitre	182. tier
33. gait	83. manege	133. rage	183. tiger
34. gaiter	84. mange	134. ragtime	184. time
35. game	85. manger	135. raiment	185. timer
36. gamer	86. mare	136. rain	186. tine
37. gamete	87. margin	137. ramie	187. tinge
38. gamier	88. marine	138. ranee	188. tire
39. gamin	89. mart	139. rang	189. train
40. gamine	90. marten	140. range	190. trainee
41. garment	91. martin	141. rani	191. tram
42. garnet	92. mate	142. rant	192. tree
43. gate	93. matinee	143. rate	193. treeing
44. gater	94. mating	144. rating	194. triage
45. gear	95. meager	145. reagent	195. trig
46. geminate	96. meagre	146. ream	196. trim
47. gene	97. mean	147. reaming	197. trine
48. genera	98. meaner	148. regain	
49. genie	99. meant	149. regent	
50. genre	100. meat	150. regime	

#59

How many words can you make from these 9 letters? There is no letter which must be used in every word. You can use only these 9 letters and a letter cannot be used more than once in any word (you may use 2 A's). It's possible to make one 9-letter word.

Score: 20 words or more – EXCELLENT

    15 words or more – VERY GOOD

    10 words or more – GOOD

It's possible to make 150 words of 3 or more letters. (See following page for answers).

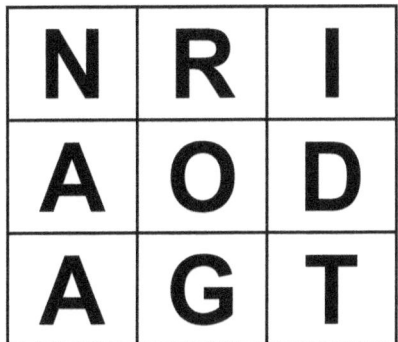

Your Answers:

1. adagio	39. dirt	77. inroad	115. rid
2. Adar	40. dog	78. into	116. rig
3. ado	41. doing	79. ion	117. rind
4. adoring	42. don	80. iota	118. ring
5. adorn	43. dong	81. iron	119. riot
6. adroit	44. dot	82. nadir	120. road
7. again	45. doting	83. nag	121. roan
8. agar	46. drag	84. naiad	122. rod
9. ago	47. dragon	85. naira	123. rot
10. agora	48. drain	86. nard	124. tad
11. aid	49. gad	87. nit	125. tag
12. air	50. Gaia	88. nod	126. Tai
13. and	51. gain	89. nor	127. taiga
14. angora	52. gait	90. not	128. Taino
15. ant	53. gar	91. oar	129. tan
16. anti	54. gator	92. oaring	130. tang
17. aorta	55. giant	93. oat	131. tango
18. argon	56. gin	94. Odin	132. tar
19. argot	57. gird	95. orating	133. taring
20. aria	58. girt	96. ordain	134. tarn
21. arid	59. gnat	97. organ	135. taro
22. art	60. goad	98. rad	136. tiara
23. atria	61. goat	99. radian	137. tin
24. dag	62. God	100. radiant	138. toad
25. Dai	63. gonad	101. radio	139. tog
26. daring	64. got	102. radon	140. toga
27. darn	65. grad	103. rag	141. ton
28. dart	66. <u>gradation</u>	104. raid	142. tor
29. darting	67. grain	105. rain	143. tori
30. data	68. grand	106. ran	144. torn
31. dating	69. grant	107. rand	145. trading
32. Diana	70. grid	108. rang	146. train
33. dig	71. grin	109. rani	147. triad
34. din	72. grind	110. rant	148. trig
35. dinar	73. grit	111. rat	149. trio
36. ding	74. groan	112. rating	150. trod
37. dingo	75. groin	113. ratio	
38. dint	76. ingot	114. ration	

#60

How many words can you make from these 9 letters? There is no letter which must be used in every word. You can use only these 9 letters and a letter cannot be used more than once in any word (you may use 2 E's). It's possible to make one 9-letter word.

Score: 20 words or more – EXCELLENT

    15 words or more – VERY GOOD

    10 words or more – GOOD

It's possible to make 136 words of 3 or more letters. (See following page for answers).

Your Answers:
_____ _____ _____
_____ _____ _____
_____ _____ _____
_____ _____ _____
_____ _____ _____
_____ _____ _____
_____ _____ _____
_____ _____ _____
_____ _____ _____
_____ _____ _____
_____ _____ _____
_____ _____ _____
_____ _____ _____
_____ _____ _____

1. ace	35. crag	69. give	103. ranee
2. acing	36. crane	70. given	104. rang
3. acne	37. crave	71. grace	105. range
4. acre	38. craven	72. grain	106. rani
5. aerie	39. craving	73. grave	107. rave
6. age	40. Cree	74. graven	108. raven
7. ager	41. cringe	75. Grecian	109. ravine
8. agree	42. eager	76. green	110. raving
9. air	43. ear	77. grievance	111. regain
10. anger	44. earing	78. grieve	112. reign
11. arc	45. earn	79. grin	113. rein
12. arcing	46. engrave	80. ice	114. rev
13. are	47. enrage	81. Inca	115. rice
14. avenge	48. envier	82. ire	116. rig
15. avenger	49. era	83. nacre	117. ring
16. aver	50. ere	84. nae	118. rive
17. cage	51. erg	85. nag	119. riven
18. cagier	52. Erie	86. naive	120. vain
19. cairn	53. eve	87. narc	121. vainer
20. can	54. even	88. nave	122. van
21. cane	55. ever	89. near	123. vane
22. caner	56. evince	90. nee	124. veer
23. car	57. gain	91. nerve	125. veering
24. care	58. gainer	92. never	126. vein
25. careen	59. gar	93. nevi	127. vena
26. caring	60. gave	94. nice	128. venae
27. carve	61. gear	95. nicer	129. venire
28. carving	62. gee	96. niece	130. verge
29. cave	63. gene	97. race	131. via
30. caver	64. genera	98. racing	132. vicar
31. cavern	65. generic	99. rag	133. vice
32. caving	66. genie	100. rage	134. vie
33. cigar	67. genre	101. rain	135. vine
34. cir	68. gin	102. ran	136. vinegar

#61

How many words can you make from these 9 letters? There is no letter which must be used in every word. You can use only these 9 letters and a letter cannot be used more than once in any word (you may use 2 E's and 2 R's). It's possible to make one 9-letter word.

Score: 20 words or more – EXCELLENT

    15 words or more – VERY GOOD

    10 words or more – GOOD

Hint: don't forget the plural forms of words, for example ear is 1 word and ears is a 2nd word. It's possible to make 161 words of 3 or more letters. (See following page for answers).

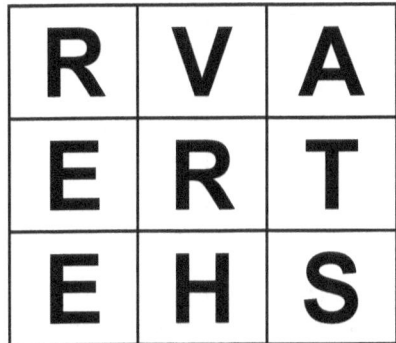

Your Answers:

1. are	42. <u>harvester</u>	83. resh	124. tare
2. Ares	43. has	84. rest	125. tares
3. arrest	44. hast	85. rester	126. tars
4. art	45. haste	86. revert	127. tea
5. arts	46. hat	87. reverts	128. tear
6. ash	47. hate	88. revs	129. tearer
7. aster	48. hater	89. rhea	130. tears
8. ate	49. hates	90. rheas	131. teas
9. aver	50. hats	91. sat	132. tease
10. avers	51. have	92. sate	133. teaser
11. averse	52. haves	93. save	134. tee
12. avert	53. hear	94. saver	135. tees
13. averts	54. hearer	95. sea	136. terse
14. ear	55. hears	96. sear	137. terser
15. ears	56. hearse	97. seat	138. the
16. earth	57. heart	98. see	139. thee
17. earths	58. hearts	99. seer	140. there
18. ease	59. heat	100. sera	141. these
19. east	60. heater	101. sere	142. three
20. Easter	61. heaters	102. serrate	143. threes
21. eat	62. heats	103. serve	144. trash
22. eater	63. heave	104. server	145. traverse
23. eats	64. heaver	105. set	146. tree
24. eaves	65. heaves	106. sever	147. trees
25. era	66. her	107. share	148. tsar
26. erase	67. here	108. sharer	149. vas
27. ere	68. hers	109. shave	150. vase
28. err	69. rare	110. shaver	151. vast
29. errs	70. rarest	111. she	152. vaster
30. Erse	71. rase	112. shear	153. vat
31. ester	72. rash	113. shearer	154. vats
32. ether	73. rasher	114. sheer	155. veer
33. ethers	74. rat	115. sheet	156. veers
34. eve	75. rate	116. star	157. verse
35. ever	76. rates	117. stare	158. vest
36. eves	77. rather	118. starer	159. Vesta
37. hare	78. rats	119. starve	160. vet
38. hares	79. rave	120. stave	161. vets
39. hart	80. raves	121. steer	
40. harts	81. rear	122. stere	
41. harvest	82. rears	123. tar	

#62

How many words can you make from these 12 letters? There is no letter which must be used in every word. You can use only these 12 letters and a letter cannot be used more than once in any word (you may use 2 O's, 2 I's and 2 T's). It's possible to make one 12-letter word.

Score: 40 words or more – EXCELLENT

30 words or more – VERY GOOD

20 words or more – GOOD

It's possible to make 207 words of 5 or more letters. (See following page for answers).

B	R	L	N
T	A	O	O
T	E	I	I

Your Answers:

1. abettor	53. bloat	105. loaner	157. rotate
2. abler	54. blotter	106. loiter	158. rotation
3. abolition	55. boater	107. loner	159. rotten
4. abort	56. boiler	108. loonier	160. table
5. abortion	57. bolero	109. looter	161. tablet
6. aileron	58. boner	110. lotion	162. taboo
7. airline	59. bonito	111. nailer	163. tabor
8. albeit	60. Boolean	112. nattier	164. tailor
9. albino	61. bootie	113. niter	165. Taino
10. alert	62. borate	114. nitrate	166. taint
11. alibi	63. boreal	115. nitre	167. talent
12. alien	64. borne	116. nitrite	168. talon
13. aline	65. boron	117. noble	169. tarot
14. alone	66. bottle	118. nobler	170. tenor
15. alter	67. bottler	119. notable	171. Teton
16. anole	68. brain	120. noter	172. tetra
17. antler	69. brant	121. oblate	173. Tibetan
18. atilt	70. Breton	122. oblation	174. tibia
19. atone	71. brine	123. obliteration	175. tibiae
20. atoner	72. Briton	124. obtain	176. tibial
21. attire	73. brittle	125. obtainer	177. tiler
22. bailer	74. broil	126. oiler	178. tilter
23. bailor	75. elation	127. oilier	179. tinier
24. bairn	76. entail	128. oolite	180. tinter
25. baiter	77. eolian	129. orate	181. titan
26. baler	78. inert	130. oration	182. titer
27. banter	79. inertia	131. orbit	183. title
28. barite	80. inertial	132. oriel	184. titre
29. baritone	81. inlet	133. orient	185. Tobit
30. baron	82. inter	134. oriental	186. toenail
31. baronet	83. irate	135. oriole	187. toiler
32. baton	84. labor	136. Orion	188. toilet
33. batten	85. latent	137. Orlon	189. tolerant
34. batter	86. later	138. ornate	190. toleration
35. battier	87. Latin	139. ottar	191. tonal
36. battle	88. Latino	140. otter	192. toner
37. battler	89. latrine	141. ratio	193. tonier
38. beano	90. latter	142. ration	194. tooter
39. betatron	91. learn	143. ratite	195. totable
40. bettor	92. learnt	144. ratline	196. total
41. biota	93. lento	145. rattle	197. toter
42. biotin	94. liane	146. relation	198. trail
43. biretta	95. libation	147. reliant	199. train
44. biter	96. Libra	148. renal	200. trait
45. bitten	97. libretti	149. rental	201. treat
46. bitter	98. libretto	150. retail	202. trial
47. bittern	99. linear	151. retain	203. tribal
48. bittier	100. liner	152. retina	204. tribe
49. blain	101. liter	153. retinal	205. trilobite
50. blare	102. literati	154. retool	206. trine
51. blear	103. litre	155. robin	207. trite
52. bleat	104. litter	156. robot	

#63

How many words can you make from these 12 letters? There is no letter which must be used in every word. You can use only these 12 letters and a letter cannot be used more than once in any word (you may use 2 O's and 2 M's). It's possible to make one 12-letter word.

Score: 40 words or more – EXCELLENT

30 words or more – VERY GOOD

20 words or more – GOOD

It's possible to make 229 words of 4 or more letters. (See following 2 pages for answers).

W	T	O	O
M	L	A	H
M	E	C	N

Your Answers:

1. ache	41. cleat	81. heat
2. acme	42. clew	82. helm
3. acne	43. clone	83. helot
4. aeon	44. clot	84. hewn
5. ahem	45. cloth	85. hole
6. aloe	46. clothe	86. home
7. alone	47. clown	87. hone
8. alto	48. coal	88. hoot
9. amen	49. coat	89. hotel
10. ammo	50. coelom	90. howl
11. anew	51. cola	91. lace
12. anole	52. colon	92. lame
13. ante	53. colt	93. lament
14. anthem	54. coma	94. lance
15. atom	55. come	95. lancet
16. atone	56. comet	96. lane
17. calm	57. comma	97. latch
18. came	58. comment	98. late
19. camel	59. common	99. lath
20. Camelot	60. commonweal	100. lathe
21. cameo	61. Commonwealth	101. lawn
22. cane	62. cone	102. leach
23. canoe	63. cool	103. lean
24. cant	64. coolant	104. lemon
25. cantle	65. coon	105. lent
26. canto	66. coot	106. lento
27. Celt	67. cote	107. loach
28. cent	68. cowl	108. loam
29. chalet	69. each	109. loan
30. chant	70. echo	110. loath
31. chat	71. enact	111. loathe
32. cheat	72. etch	112. locate
33. chemo	73. ethanol	113. loch
34. chew	74. hale	114. loco
35. chon	75. halo	115. lone
36. chow	76. halt	116. loom
37. clam	77. hamlet	117. loon
38. clan	78. haole	118. loot
39. claw	79. hate	119. loth
40. clean	80. heal	120. mace

121. mach
122. macho
123. male
124. malt
125. mane
126. manhole
127. mantel
128. mantle
129. match
130. mate
131. math
132. meal
133. mean
134. meant
135. meat
136. melon
137. melt
138. memo
139. mental
140. menthol
141. meow
142. metal
143. methanol
144. moan
145. moat
146. mocha
147. mole
148. molt
149. molten
150. moment
151. Monel
152. mono
153. monocle
154. month
155. mooch
156. moon
157. moot

158. mote
159. motel
160. moth
161. mown
162. nacho
163. name
164. neat
165. newt
166. noel
167. notch
168. note
169. oath
170. ocean
171. ocelot
172. octal
173. octane
174. oleo
175. Olmec
176. omen
177. once
178. onto
179. owlet
180. taco
181. talc
182. tale
183. talon
184. tame
185. teach
186. teal
187. team
188. Tewa
189. than
190. thane
191. thaw
192. them
193. then
194. thew

195. toea
196. tome
197. tonal
198. tone
199. tool
200. towel
201. town
202. wahoo
203. wale
204. wane
205. want
206. watch
207. watchmen
208. weal
209. wealth
210. wean
211. welch
212. welt
213. wench
214. went
215. whale
216. wham
217. what
218. wheat
219. whelm
220. when
221. whet
222. whoa
223. whole
224. whom
225. woman
226. women
227. wont
228. wool
229. woolen

This page intentionally left blank.

#64

How many words can you make from these 12 letters? Every word must contain the letter "I". You can use only these 12 letters and a letter cannot be used more than once in any word (you may use 2 N's and 2 I's). It's possible to make one 12-letter word.

Score: 40 words or more – EXCELLENT

    30 words or more – VERY GOOD

    20 words or more – GOOD

It's possible to make 223 words of 4 or more letters. (See following 2 pages for answers).

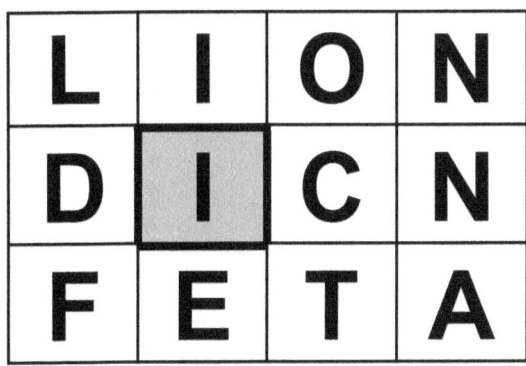

Your Answers:

1. acid	41. confidant	81. fail
2. aconite	42. confide	82. failed
3. actin	43. <u>confidential</u>	83. fain
4. actinide	44. confine	84. faint
5. action	45. confined	85. fainted
6. afield	46. contain	86. fancied
7. aide	47. contained	87. feint
8. ailed	48. defiant	88. Fenian
9. alien	49. deficit	89. fetid
10. aline	50. defoliant	90. fiat
11. alined	51. deli	91. fiction
12. alit	52. deltaic	92. fictional
13. ancient	53. deltic	93. field
14. anilin	54. denial	94. fiend
15. aniline	55. dentin	95. file
16. anion	56. dentinal	96. filed
17. anionic	57. detail	97. filet
18. annelid	58. detain	98. final
19. anoint	59. dial	99. finale
20. anointed	60. dialect	100. finance
21. antic	61. diatonic	101. financed
22. canine	62. dice	102. find
23. cannoli	63. dicot	103. fine
24. cedi	64. dicta	104. fined
25. ciao	65. diction	105. finial
26. cilia	66. dictional	106. finite
27. ciliate	67. diet	107. Finn
28. ciliated	68. dilate	108. finned
29. citadel	69. dine	109. flint
30. cite	70. dint	110. flit
31. cited	71. docile	111. foci
32. client	72. edict	112. foetid
33. coati	73. edit	113. foil
34. coif	74. edition	114. foiled
35. coifed	75. elation	115. iced
36. coil	76. elicit	116. icon
37. coiled	77. entail	117. idea
38. coin	78. eolian	118. ideal
39. coined	79. facile	119. ideation
40. coital	80. faction	120. identical

121. idiot
122. idle
123. idol
124. ilea
125. inaction
126. inane
127. Inca
128. incident
129. incidental
130. incite
131. incited
132. incline
133. inclined
134. indent
135. Indian
136. Indic
137. indicate
138. indict
139. indite
140. indolent
141. infant
142. infantile
143. infect
144. infidel
145. infield
146. inflate
147. inflated
148. inflation
149. inflect
150. inflection
151. inflict
152. inflicted
153. info
154. infold
155. inlaid

156. inland
157. inlet
158. intend
159. inti
160. into
161. intone
162. intoned
163. iodine
164. iota
165. italic
166. ladino
167. laid
168. lain
169. Latin
170. Latino
171. liane
172. lice
173. licit
174. lidocaine
175. lied
176. lief
177. lien
178. life
179. lift
180. lifted
181. linden
182. line
183. lined
184. linen
185. linnet
186. lint
187. lion
188. loci
189. loin
190. loti

191. nail
192. nailed
193. nation
194. niacin
195. nice
196. nicotine
197. nine
198. notice
199. noticed
200. notified
201. Odin
202. oilcan
203. oiled
204. oldie
205. Oneida
206. tail
207. tailed
208. tailfin
209. Taino
210. tidal
211. tide
212. tied
213. tilde
214. tile
215. tiled
216. tine
217. tined
218. tinfoil
219. tinned
220. toenail
221. toil
222. toiled
223. tonic

This page intentionally left blank.

#65

How many words can you make from these 12 letters? Every word must contain the letter "E". You can use only these 12 letters and a letter cannot be used more than once in any word (you may use 2 E's and 2 A's). It's possible to make one 12-letter word.

Score: 40 words or more – EXCELLENT

    30 words or more – VERY GOOD

    20 words or more – GOOD

Hint: don't forget the plural forms of words, for example arena is 1 word and arenas is a 2nd word. It's possible to make 340 words of 5 or more letters. Thirty-three words contain the letter "X". (See following two pages for answers).

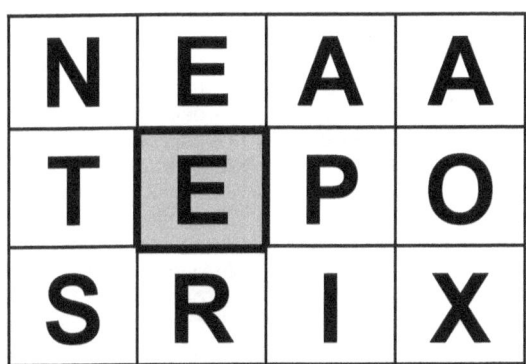

Your Answers:

1. Aeneas	48. entropies	95. noise	142. Penates
2. aerate	49. eosin	96. Norse	143. penes
3. aerates	50. epoxies	97. nosier	144. penis
4. aerie	51. erase	98. notaries	145. pentose
5. aeries	52. Eries	99. noter	146. peonies
6. anapest	53. Esperanto	100. notes	147. perinea
7. anise	54. esprit	101. onset	148. peritonea
8. anorexia	55. ester	102. opens	149. Persian
9. Antares	56. exasperation	103. opera	150. person
10. antes	57. exert	104. operate	151. persona
11. antisera	58. exerts	105. operates	152. personae
12. antsier	59. exist	106. opiate	153. pertain
13. aortae	60. exits	107. opiates	154. pertains
14. apexes	61. expanse	108. opine	155. peseta
15. apnea	62. expert	109. opines	156. pester
16. apnoea	63. experts	110. orate	157. pesto
17. apnoeas	64. expiate	111. orates	158. peter
18. areas	65. expiates	112. orient	159. peters
19. arena	66. expiator	113. orients	160. piaster
20. arenas	67. expire	114. ornate	161. piastre
21. Aries	68. expires	115. osier	162. piers
22. arise	69. export	116. paean	163. pines
23. arisen	70. exports	117. paeans	164. pintoes
24. arose	71. expose	118. painter	165. pioneer
25. Asante	72. extensor	119. painters	166. pioneers
26. aspen	73. extra	120. paise	167. pirate
27. aspirate	74. extras	121. panes	168. pirates
28. aspire	75. inept	122. pantie	169. poets
29. aster	76. inert	123. panties	170. pointer
30. astern	77. inexpert	124. pantries	171. pointers
31. atone	78. insert	125. parasite	172. poise
32. atoner	79. inset	126. parent	173. pones
33. atones	80. instep	127. parents	174. ponies
34. atropine	81. inter	128. pares	175. pontes
35. earnest	82. interpose	129. parse	176. poser
36. earns	83. inters	130. parties	177. poster
37. easier	84. irate	131. paseo	178. postern
38. Easter	85. naperies	132. paste	179. poxes
39. eastern	86. nares	133. pastern	180. praise
40. eaten	87. nastier	134. pastier	181. prate
41. eater	88. nearest	135. paten	182. prates
42. enter	89. nears	136. patens	183. praxes
43. enters	90. neater	137. pates	184. preen
44. entire	91. niter	138. pears	185. preens
45. entrap	92. niters	139. peasant	186. preexist
46. entraps	93. nitre	140. peens	187. present
47. entries	94. nixes	141. peers	188. preset

189. presto	227. retinas	265. sniper	303. tares
190. pries	228. retsina	266. snore	304. taxer
191. priest	229. rinse	267. soapier	305. taxes
192. prise	230. ripen	268. soiree	306. taxies
193. pronate	231. ripens	269. sortie	307. tears
194. pronates	232. ripest	270. spare	308. tease
195. prone	233. riposte	271. spate	309. teaser
196. prose	234. risen	272. spear	310. teens
197. protean	235. rites	273. spent	311. tenor
198. protein	236. ropes	274. spine	312. tenors
199. proxies	237. roseate	275. spinet	313. tense
200. raise	238. rotes	276. spiraea	314. tenser
201. ranee	239. saner	277. spire	315. tensor
202. ranees	240. Santee	278. spirea	316. terns
203. rapes	241. sapient	279. spite	317. terse
204. rapine	242. sarape	280. spore	318. tiers
205. rapines	243. sateen	281. spree	319. tines
206. rates	244. satire	282. sprite	320. tires
207. reaps	245. seaport	283. stainer	321. toner
208. reason	246. seatrain	284. stare	322. toners
209. reins	247. seine	285. steep	323. tones
210. rents	248. seiner	286. steer	324. tonier
211. repast	249. senate	287. stein	325. toper
212. repeat	250. senator	288. steno	326. topers
213. repeats	251. senior	289. stere	327. Tories
214. repent	252. sente	290. stereo	328. trainee
215. repents	253. separate	291. stern	329. trainees
216. repine	254. separation	292. sterna	330. traipse
217. repines	255. sepia	293. stoae	331. treason
218. repose	256. septa	294. stone	332. trees
219. resent	257. serape	295. stoner	333. trepan
220. resin	258. serpent	296. stonier	334. trepans
221. resonate	259. sexier	297. store	335. tries
222. respite	260. siren	298. striae	336. trine
223. retain	261. sixteen	299. stripe	337. trines
224. retains	262. snare	300. taper	338. tripe
225. retina	263. sneer	301. tapers	339. trope
226. retinae	264. snipe	302. tapes	340. tropes

This page intentionally left blank.

ABOUT THE AUTHOR

Daniel Wieczorek was born in 1947 in Ionia, Michigan. He graduated from the University of Michigan with a B.S. in Forestry in 1969. He moved to Oregon to work in the field of forestry in 1971. That was followed by a move to Alaska in 1975, where he continued his career in forestry. After about a 14 year career in forestry, Daniel decided to do something different and he served as a Peace Corps Volunteer in The Philippines from 1985 – 1987. Upon completion of his Peace Corps service he returned to Alaska, where he attended the University of Alaska – Fairbanks and received an M.B.A. in 1991. This was followed by a move to South Korea in 1992, where Daniel taught English to Korean people wishing to improve their English Language skills. Daniel's next stop was in New York City, where he worked as temporary staff at Deutsche Bank from 1998 – 2001. He left NYC in March 2001 and moved on to his present home in Mitaka City, Tokyo, Japan. He is teaching English in Japan and at this time he's been teaching as a career for about 17 years. He has been hiking, climbing and doing photography since he was about 12 years old.